THE GOOD, THE BAD, AND THE ADORABLE

My First Year as a Father

SEAN M. TEAFORD

authorHOUSE®

AuthorHouse™
1663 Liberty Drive
Bloomington, IN 47403
www.authorhouse.com
Phone: 1 (800) 839-8640

Published by AuthorHouse   02/26/2016

ISBN: 978-1-5049-8061-6 (sc)
ISBN: 978-1-5049-8062-3 (e)

Library of Congress Control Number: 2016902990

Print information available on the last page.

This book is printed on acid-free paper.

For my wife and my son

Acknowledgements

The most important person that I need to thank for making this collection of essays a reality is my wife who not only gave birth to our son but allowed me to write about many of our experiences throughout the year. It certainly has not been the easiest experience but thanks to her immeasurable strength we have made it through our first year as parents.

Of course, the other person that needs to be thanked is my son who has provided his parents with comfort, joy, headaches, and sleepless nights since the day he joined us in this world. There have been countless days when his smile made things just a little easier for both of us.

Lastly, I would like to thank my family, friends, followers, and occasional readers of my blog, Time To Keep It Simple, where these short essays were first published. It has been a tremendous experience sharing this journey with you all.

Other Works By Sean M. Teaford

Teaching A Stone To Talk: Nature Poems (Bending Tree Press, 2003)

Kaddish Diary (Pudding House Publications, 2005)

Paintings In Under A Thousand Words: Nature Poems (Author House, 2016)

What Was Not Said: Echoes From The Holocaust (Author House, 2016)

Out On The Limbs: Searching For Answers In The Family Tree (Author House, 2016)

CONTENTS

2016:
WE MADE IT!

INTRODUCTION

I originally started my blog, Time To Keep It Simple, in May of 2013 as a means to simply continue writing without the strictures of keeping to a particular topic or form. Hence, the title that I chose for this new endeavor. The only parameters that I set for myself were that each daily post had to be at least 400 words in length.

Over time, there were subjects that seemed to come up naturally and that I truly enjoyed writing about. Not surprisingly, when my wife and I found out that we were expecting a baby, this became the topic about which I was most passionate about and an experience, as a father expecting his first child, that I wanted to share with everyone.

After our son was born I found myself having conversations with other parents about some of the interesting things that we should anticipate happening during the first year. I had not heard about any of these antidotes before and so I wanted to start writing more regularly about these usually humorous occurrences.

Arranged chronologically, this book is a collection of both those early posts of doctor appointments and preparations for arrival as well as the more interesting moments that I experienced during my first year as a father.

2014:
It's Not A Moonscape!

July 22: Not Just Another Day Out Of The Office

This time last week I left the office in the middle of the day to go to a doctor's appointment. While the timing was not ideal, it was the only appointment that worked in both our schedules. Fortunately, everyone at my office knows that I only schedule things in the middle of the day if there is no other option available so they were fine with me leaving at two. Honestly, I don't know how I would have gotten over it if I was not there to see the first pictures of our baby. Yes, you read that correctly, I am going to be a father.

While we had the tests done to confirm the previous week, this first ultrasound is a completely different experience when you see the fast flicker of the heart on the screen. It is an instantaneous bond that most have experienced but no one has been able to accurately express. It is a life changing moment that makes you reconsider your perspective of the world around you. For some, their views change but as for me, to my surprise, that moment solidified every perspective that I have ever expressed (at least those in recent years). In fact, I am glad that I have continued to write as I want my child to look back and really know who I am (like Michael Keaton in "My Life" except I am not dying anytime soon).

Above all, it is an immense feeling of excitement and fear. I am excited to see our child, teach them about life, share with them the things that I have learned in my limited years, and make sure that they don't make the mistakes, of which there are too many to list, that I have in my life. I am also fearful of falling short as a father and for the simple fact that I am now responsible for another human being on this earth and that I must do everything in my power to protect my child and keep them safe. Simply put, I worry that my child will not look at me the same way that I look at my dad.

We have seen and heard a wide variety of reactions to this news (it's not a picture of a moonscape) and we have tried to soak it all up as the experience washed over us like a tsunami. But, even though it is sometimes difficult to process moment to moment, it is a time that I will never forget especially when I was able to see my mom's face when she realized why it would take eight months before her birthday present would arrive. And, just think, this is only the first of many moments that I will carry with me for the rest of my life.

July 24: Time Flies
When I'm Thinking

Last night I had planned on going to bed early. Around ten, I sat at my desk to clean out some receipts from my wallet and throw them in the shred box. This is a simple task that should have taken no more than ten minutes. However, I found myself sitting there, staring at the wall, and thinking. A very dangerous habit but one that I can't seem to break. Before I knew it, midnight had come and gone and I was just getting ready for bed.

Since the moment we found out that we are having a baby there have been moments here and there when I would catch a glimpse of how drastically our life would change. Last night was the first time when I really sat and thought about all that needs to be done and everything that we will have to shift around in our life. While time is one consideration, space is another and as I looked around our office, there are a lot of things that need to be changed by the end of the year.

It is nothing that we can't handle but it is going to take some thought to plan out the moves necessary to maximize the limited square footage of our apartment. What can I say, we have a lot of stuff. But that is part of the process; that is part of the change that occurs during this stage in life; out with our stuff, in with the baby stuff. It makes me wonder what George Carlin would have to say about this change in stuff status.

Contrary to what you might be thinking, it is kind of a relief. While there are a lot of things that we will be holding on to, it brings to my attention all the things that we never should have held on to in the first place. We're not hoarders but we are not living a minimalistic life either. It reminds me of when we decided to move to Israel; we had to look around and figure out what we really wanted to keep and what we could get rid of. While this is not as extreme, we now need to focus on what things we want to take with us on this new adventure.

So now, in addition to the cleaning that is already long overdue, it is time to sort and organize so that we can begin preparing for the life that we have always dreamed of which is now, slowly, becoming a reality. I am sure that there will be times when the stress will outweigh the optimism but, overall, these moments when I am just able to sit and think quietly are the ones that will continue to fuel my anticipation. In between, I am going to continue working, cleaning, organizing, and trying my best to prepare myself for the changes on the horizon.

July 27: Great Conversations And Unwanted "Advice"

Ever since we announced that we were having a baby there have been dozens and dozens of family and friends offering us advice based on their experience. I am a firm proponent of gathering as much information as possible from as many people as possible especially from those who are parents. We have already had a variety of great conversations and have received a tremendous amount of excellent advice since the announcement and we are constantly receiving little bits of wisdom every now and again. It is amazing how much love and support that we have received and we are grateful for those people in our life. Yesterday was one of those days when we felt that warmth as family continuously approached us, offered their congratulations, and chatted briefly with my wife about how she is holding up.

Of course, over the past couple of weeks, there have also been a few people that keep popping up and offering lectures of what we should be doing and what we are currently doing wrong. They have also offered their pessimistic views on what they "hope doesn't happen" while mixing in monologues about how we can avoid unrelated problems that they know absolutely nothing about. This is usually followed by "offers" to gain some additional practice in the coming months because we have obviously never been around infants and know nothing about some of the unpleasant aspects which they proceed to outline in great detail.

These people have a commonality… they are clearly the center of the world. It is not a dialogue, it is a matter of they know what is best and we need to do it that way or we are wrong. This characteristic also encompasses a few people that are not excited about the good news because that means that we are not able to give them as much of our attention anymore. Did I mention that these people are over five years old?

This is a very special time in our life and we want to embrace all the positive energy, unique experiences, and great people in our life. While, for various reasons, we can't get rid of all the negative people and energy, we will do our best to minimize them and focus on the love and support. And, of course, we won't turn down great advice now and again!

AUGUST 4: HEARTBEAT

We woke up this morning still on vacation, not having to go to work, and no detailed schedule ahead of us but with plenty of things that needed to get done. The first of these things was to drive back home.

After a quick breakfast in the Holiday Inn lobby we packed everything up, got in the car, and slowly made our way from detour to detour the first of which was up the street from the hotel at Ollie's Bargain Outlet in Shamokin Dam where we were able to again introduce my parents to someplace new. With a few bargains in our bags and water in hand, we made our way back to the highway so we could make some serious progress.

Having driven on I-80 earlier in the summer I knew we were about 2 ½ hours away from home but, with the only item on our calendar not scheduled until 6:30, we had plenty of time to stop again. This time we got out to stretch at Country Junction in Lehighton. While my wife and I had been their once before, this was again a new place for my parents. Sometimes it is the small interesting places that are the best to stop and stretch at in the middle of a long drive.

The rest of the drive was uneventful and uncongested and as we got closer to the final exit of our trip we made a split decision to go to a restaurant for lunch that we have ever been to, Avenue Kitchen in Villanova. While the food and service was good I couldn't help but take note of the fact that the check for just lunch (and this was moderately priced for the Main Line) was more than what we spent for lunch and dinner combined the day before during our Knoebels adventure.

We got back to my parents' house by midafternoon with plenty of time for us to relax before heading over to the doctor's office. While it was nice to sit down and just take a bit of time away from work for the day I found myself eager to do something while anticipating the appointment that evening. No surprise, we got to the office early and waited as patiently as we could to be seen. Without a doubt, while annoying, the waiting was well worth it as for the first time we heard the tiny (and fast) heartbeat of our child, a rhythm that we will not soon forget. And, while simple, it sounds much better than Don Johnson!

AUGUST 21: THAT'S MY CHILD!

Early this morning I couldn't help but quote the Big Bopper when I saw the picture come into focus. Before our eyes, we saw the profile of our baby slowly take shape as the woman moved the ultrasound around my wife's stomach. What a drastic change from what we saw just five weeks ago!

We were still a little dumbfounded as they began measuring and checking all that they could in the image to make sure that our little one was progressing normally. Given their parents, this might be the only time in their life that they are considered normal. After these initial still shots, it was time for baby to have a little fun. Yes, it turns out that baby likes to mess with people just like daddy.

Throughout the process, the baby was moving around and having fun in their little rent free dwelling. When it came time for some more pictures that required the baby to be in a certain position it decided to do their own thing... we could hear the doctor talking, asking the baby to lay on its back followed by a slight nudge with the scanner.

Baby did exactly what you think it did, it rolled onto its belly. It took numerous attempts and a few minutes before the baby rolled all the way around. This is when we could really see the profile and see the face of our child. Five or six still frames later the doctor was almost done but baby had enough. Baby raised their arm, either to wave bye or make their first attempt at giving someone the finger, and rolled over again. That's my child!

That was the end of our visit for today and I will say that this was the best reason to roll out of bed early. Even groggy, it was an exciting morning for the two of us and another day that we will never forget (at least until we are old and senile). Now we just have to wait for some blood work and come back for some more family photos in a couple months... I guess my wife knows what she is getting for her birthday this year!

Twelve weeks in, the baby is healthy and the reality is really starting to settle in. While I was never in denial, seeing a much more developed picture of our child really hit home and has me both a little concerned about our living and financial situation but also eager to meet him or her (I still think it is a boy). It has been quite an early morning and a really long day of thinking.

October 18: It's A...

My wife and I pulled into the hospital parking lot a little later than we were expecting. It wasn't a matter of choice as traffic was particularly bad this past week. We were both especially eager to get into the building and excited to see our baby again. After all, this was the ultrasound appointment that everyone has been asking about in one way or another and we had been waiting for this appointment for some time. Of course, the day finally came and we both got held up before leaving for the hospital and slowed down on our way there. That seems to be the case for many of our appointments.

Thankfully, the office was very understanding when we called to let them know of our delay and they greeted us warmly upon seeing us walk up to the front desk. It wasn't long before we were sitting in front of the ultrasound monitor seeing our child kicking and punching the crap out of Mommy. While it was a little odd for me to watch it was even stranger for my wife as she could both see and feel the baby hit her stomach.

We sat there in awe of our child as measurement after measurement was taken and they checked the development. We watched the screen as image after image was captured and they confirmed the health and development time and again. Everything was progressing as it should when we heard a little chuckle from behind the screen. This was quickly followed with the question of whether we wanted to know the sex.

As it turns out, our baby passed the winkie test.

Our little baby boy, my son, is happy and healthy. He is an active little baby a day ahead of schedule. While I would have been happy no matter the sex of our child, knowing that we are having a boy did bring me a sense of relief. I would have loved our child no matter what but I know what it is like to be a little boy and I am looking forward to every moment that I can share that experience with my son. I have a feeling that my wife would have felt the same way if we had found out it was a girl.

Everything suddenly became a little more real in that moment. We will soon have a son. I will soon have a little boy who will carry on the family name. I am more nervous than I ever thought I would be but I think I am now ready to be a father. And, as an added bonus, my sister now owes me five dollars!

October 21: Baby Errands

On Sunday my wife and I had to get out of the apartment. With everything that has been going on lately we haven't had much time to run a few errands... they just kept getting pushed back week after week. Finally we made it to the mall and started hopping from store to store picking up the items we needed. Nothing fancy just a few items of clothing, a very important pillow, and some additional footwear.

The largest part of our outing was our trip to Babies "R" Us which ate up about two hours of our afternoon. While we did find a few items that we could purchase (clearance combined with coupon was a deal we couldn't pass up) the primary purpose of our store visit was to fill out our baby registry (which is not fun if you try to do it online). That's right, for the first time since our wedding, we walked up and down the aisles, scanner in hand, doing our best to spend other people's money (no, we didn't run into Danny DeVito).

With memories of our wedding excursions resurfacing in our minds, we were not looking forward to the process. However, once we started scanning, we couldn't help but enjoy the idea that we were picking things out not for ourselves but for our son. That was the turning point in the whole process as we kept on finding item after item that we wanted to buy for our baby.

Of course, there were a few things that weren't as simple as point and scan and there were a couple of items that we will have to research further before adding to the list. Strollers and car seats took some time while monitors were put off for another day. And while we chose some outfits, there is still a lot of clothes that need to be added before that could even come close to being a complete list. Toys were another item (except for a few stuffed animals) that we are holding off on.

By the end of the registry marathon, we had made a pretty big dent. All the furniture has been selected, travel items were put on the list, and every other category in the store supplied checklist had at least a few items selected (including a crap load of diapers - pun intended). Also added were the handful of items that we purchased that day… always remember to do this as you enjoy the registry benefits on things that you are purchasing, namely cash back.

So my son should have a pretty good start and this should prevent us from having to bring back piles of merchandise to return and/or exchange. That is the theory. And now my wife and I no longer have the aversion to registries that we previously had as things are different now that we are no longer picking out items for ourselves (okay some of the items were more for us). While we aren't quite ready for our son to be born we are at least making progress and feel like we have made one more preparation for his arrival.

OCTOBER 25: CONSIDERING THE INEVITABLE FUTURE

With the baby on the way and everything else that has been going on my wife and I have been thinking about preparing for the future. While there have been many happy moments and times of celebration, there are a few realities that we must address in order for us to not have to think about certain things and unpleasant possibilities. It is with this in mind that we have started discussing putting a will together.

This is a conversation that we had when we first got married and we simply put it aside for a number of years. It wasn't something that we would think about on a regular basis so it was simply forgotten about. Lately, it has been a thought permeating our minds and we have had to give serious consideration to many of the details.

There is nothing that has officially be done at this point... it has merely been discussion and the floating of ideas and scenarios. And while we don't have much it would be nice to get some of the broad strokes out of the way before this important project is put off again. While I don't see us forgetting about it like we previously did, we would both rather have it done now while we are motivated to do so and while we have a small measure of time to commit to this undertaking.

We have both seen and read a few wills in our lives but we never sat down to write one ourselves. But it is not just about us anymore, we want to make sure that our son (and any future children) are not left with a cluster when we are no longer around whether that is five or fifty years from now. It is also an opportunity to decide what will happen if we were to become ill toward the end and what needs to be done while we are still 'alive'.

How will the minimalistic 'estate' be handled? Who would care for our kid(s) if it, G-d forbid, happens sooner rather than later? What happens to all of our crap? What are our last wishes? What life saving measures, if any, should be taken? Where will we be planted?

Those are just some of the basic questions that we have been asking ourselves and while we don't have any definitive answers we are working things through and doing our best to write them down. While this attempt will be a broad one at best (we are doing this ourselves) it will be the basis for when we sit down with a lawyer in the future and pull everything together as it should be. We are going to take care of the basics now and work out many of the details over time. But, it is nice to know that something is getting recorded and that things will, for the most part, be taken care of and we generally know what will happen when that day comes.

October 26: Learning How To Get Back Up

I was never a particularly tough child. I remember complaining and crying when I got hurt and not wanting to push through minor injuries when participating in sports or playing with friends. While not as bad as some that I can remember, I was by no means a tough child. I learned how and enjoyed pushing through injuries later in my youth but it took some time and a bit of determination to overcome the weaknesses I had when I was smaller (I can't say that I was ever actually 'small').

Over the years however, I have built up a tolerance for pain that is a bit baffling to some and considered stupid by others. From broken bones and dislocated joints to kidney stones and fighting Fibromyalgia, I have experienced all kinds of pain and only stopped when it was preventing me from living. I've set bones, popped joints back into place, put duct tape over large cuts, and simply walked things off when they really started to hurt. Up to that point I would keep pushing and pushing until finally I had no other choice than to give in and let myself heal. Of course, for the truly minor things like bad ankle sprains, dislocations, cold/flu, and migraines it was better to keep going and work my way through them.

This is the kind of thing that I want to instill in my son. Not to the extent that I have taken it but I don't want him to let the small things stop him. Bumps and bruises are a part of living life especially when you are young and I want our son to enjoy every moment of growing up while he can. With that said, we have to do our part to let him fall and let him scrape his knees so that he can learn that it really isn't that bad. Of course, we will always be there when he needs us but some things he is going to have to learn just by doing and experiencing.

All that we can really do is guide him and try to set him up for the long life ahead of him. Bumps (and bruises) are just minor things that happen along the way but you can't just stop everything that you are doing when they happen. Life is still going on around you and if you take a break, there are potential memories that you will be missing. I guess you could say that I want to make sure that we instill in our son adversity as it has served us both incredibly well in our own lives. Hopefully we can get that message through to him early on… the same lesson that my parents tried teaching me which didn't take hold until much later in my life.

October 30: Great Way To End The Work Day

Yesterday was a busy day at the office with various events and new projects that we have to prepare for. It is a long and sometimes stressful experience but also something that we can be proud of once everything comes to pass. As the long day wound down I slowly packed my bags, closed my computer, headed out the door, and off to my next appointment. These days, these appointment, are ones that I continue looking forward to as the weeks slowly drift by. It is time to check in on the baby.

My wife and I both arrived at the doctor's office early and after catching up a bit on everything that is going on and discussing the questions that we wanted to ask the doctor we made our way through the doors, checked in, and sat in the waiting room. Every visit there seems to be a certain amount of excitement coupled with a slight hint of nervousness. It is safe to say that the worrying starts before the baby arrives.

It wasn't long before we were escorted back into an examining room (amid glares from all the pregnant women who were sitting there when we first walked in). After a quick weight and blood pressure check it was time to hear one of the most calming, if not the most calming, sound that we have in our lives at this moment... our son's heartbeat. It is a sound that fills the room (especially now that it is so much easier to find) and one that makes me look forward to the day when I will finally be able to hold him.

The tranquil moment passed as the nurse headed out the door and we waited for the doctor to appear. Again, a perfect time to make sure we had all our questions ready. The doctor came in, took some measurements, and let us know that our baby boy was perfectly healthy... all tests have come back negative, heart rate is normal, and the measurements are right where they need to be. Essentially, our kid is probably never going to be this 'normal' again.

Once we silently reveled in the good news of a quick moment, we began posing all of the questions that we have been reviewing for days. All of the 'let's just double check with the doctor' type of questions. The doctor took her time, answered all of the questions that we had, and let us know about what we should expect during the next appointment in 4 weeks. I'm sure we will have more questions for the doctor upon our return but, for now, everything is progressing as it should and we are looking forward to meeting our happy and healthy (and VERY active) little boy.

November 25: A Long Baby Appointment

For the past several months we have been seeing the doctor every four weeks to check in and make sure our son is on schedule. Last night was the last appointment in that particular schedule as we will now be heading to the doctor every two or three weeks until our son's birthday. Thankfully, everything has checked out so far and he is developing close to what the doctor expects (he is actually a week ahead of schedule at this point).

However, while the baby is progressing as planned, the doctor was running late last night… very late. We both made our way to the office a little quicker than expected and checked in at the front desk about twenty five minutes early. Once a couple of seats opened up in the waiting room we settled in for the duration as given the mass of people in the office we knew there was no way that they would be running on time. Our appointment time came and went with little expectation as to when we would be seen.

Jeopardy kept us occupied for a little while but our patience began slowly dissolving as Wheel of Fortune gradually killed our brain cells. By the time that show ended there were still a few of us fidgeting in the waiting room and what little patience was left quickly vanished once Dancing With The Stars came on. Honestly, I don't know how people can watch that show. Fortunately, it wasn't long after the dancing started when we heard my wife's name being called and we moved as fast as we could to the examining room.

This change in scenery was met with more waiting as we could hear the doctors and nurses scurrying up and down the hallways like mice trying to escape from a trash can. This was accompanied by the sounds of heartbeats from the adjacent rooms. It was nearly 8:30 when the doctor finally opened the door, listened to the heart rate, took the usual measurements, and answered a couple of questions that we had for her. We discussed the next appointment and were on our way out having waited over two hours for a ten minute appointment.

It was a long night that followed a long day but it was well worth the wait as we were able to once again hear our son and watch him kick as he wondered why he was being poked and prodded. Like many nights, that is what grounds us. But we also learned the important lesson to never again make a doctor appointment the week of Thanksgiving… I think even the baby was not happy about having to sit in the waiting room so long.

December 11: Ahead Of Schedule

Now that my wife is in her third trimester we are scheduling doctor appointments for every two weeks. The last time that we were in the office we had quite the wait as couples crammed in one last appointment before Thanksgiving and many of the doctors had already headed out for the holiday. Last night was much better as we were shown back to the examining room a few minutes ahead of our appointment time.

After enjoying hearing our son's heartbeat, it was time for the doctor to come in and take some measurements. As it turns out, at 28 1/2 weeks my wife is measuring 31 weeks. With very little weight gain to speak of, it is safe to say that our baby is a wee bit ahead of schedule. This also explains the discomfort and sometimes pain that my wife has been experiencing lately and her inability to sleep throughout the night.

Now that he is so far along, it is fun to play with him from time to time. He knows both of our voices and can feel each time that we rub him usually poking or kicking our hands. He is surprisingly active during the day and even into the night after I get home from work. I like to think that he waits up to hear daddy but I know that is not realistic.

Even though we have not been able to find the right name for our son we do have a couple of options that we have been keeping to ourselves. However, it is safe to say that Deuteronomy, Percy, and Junior have been eliminated from contention. While we would like to have a few options selected beforehand it is probably going to come down to what comes to mind when we see our son for the first time. Maybe that time will be sooner than expected.

This is a little different of an approach than one of the brothers from the lodge. He and his wife had the named picked out for their daughter months ago in anticipation of today actually. Sometimes you just come across the one name that just fits and you stick with it… of course, we already have a name picked out for a girl but that is not helping us at all right now. Of course, at the same time, we are not going to let ourselves fall into the Paul and Jamie conundrum either.

It will all take care of itself in time. It is just a matter of how much time we will have to think about his name. So far it looks like we are having that timeframe cut down by 2 ½ weeks. I guess we will have to keep thinking of options as we continue looking forward to his arrival.

December 15: Birthing Class, Pizza, And A Hospital Visit

Having gotten up early the day before and being out of the apartment all day, Sunday was not a fun experience getting out of bed. But we had good reason for an early rise as we were off to class yesterday! We had signed up for the birthing class about a month ago and opted for the one day variety instead of the multi-week long process that just doesn't agree with either of our schedules at this point.

A little sluggish and having been held up by anything and everything along the way, we were the last ones to arrive but thankfully the class had only started a couple minutes prior to our arrival. Obviously, we jumped right in as soon as we were able to take our coats off and take a seat. Another new experience during this new adventure.

The class went well offering up a lot of information and answering numerous questions that everyone had. It was led by one of the nurses from Bryn Mawr Hospital whom you could tell was well versed in fielding all of the different questions that new parents have. While the class was interesting it was a little repetitive and the warm room did not mix well with the lack of sleep from the prior week. I did stay awake and attentive but there were a few touch and go moments here and there.

Halfway through we all left to get some lunch with a time set to resume the educational portion of the day. I didn't have to say much knowing that my wife would probably like to go to Peace of Pizza. Not surprisingly, we found the majority of the class at the counter ordering their meals when we walked in the door.

There were also a number of families there for lunch with gaggles of young kids circling them like hyper sharks. We didn't think anything of it and smiled at the situation before taking another few bites. However, my wife and I were amused when we saw the looks of terror on the faces of our classmates. I guess they weren't quite ready for the dose of reality.

We returned to the class and finished up the sitting portion of the day with a few games that brought a little perspective to the situation. After these were completed we got back in the car and we all met at the hospital for a tour of labor and delivery. While those terrified looks seemed to creep back onto many of their faces I could feel the two of us getting more and more excited (and more nervous). Time is going so fast and it won't be very long before we return expecting to leave as a family of three.

December 20: 3-D Baby

Thursday was a hectic day but hectic in a good way as the early morning was a filled with coffee and anticipation at seeing our son again. It was almost as if he knew he was going to have his picture taken that morning. He was squirming from the moment we got out of bed and was pushing closer to the surface trying to get just a little bit closer.

He was calm for a time and very active at other points in the morning. Once the ultrasound began, he seemed to both want his picture taken and wanted nothing to do with the process at the same time. Of course, like the rest of the men in my family, he had his hands up and ready to block his face.

Even with all of the moving around, kicking, and punching, the nurse was able to take all the measurements that she needed… more than enough to tell us that our son is developing normally and maybe a little bit ahead of schedule. She was also able to catch him in the middle of one of his shifts with his face uncovered taking a nice 3-D image of our baby. A second later and he put his hands back up and didn't move them away for the rest of the morning.

And now we have a face without a name. The latter will come in time but, for now, we know he takes after my side of the family both in his mannerisms and some of his facial features. And, yes, he still listens to daddy when I ask him to move, kick, etc. I am going to enjoy his cooperation while it lasts!

The doctor soon followed and double checked everything that had just been done and all the measurements that had been taken. Thankfully, everything was confirmed and our son is expected to be approximately 8 ½ pounds by the time his birthday comes around. While a big baby, we were expecting this as I was about the same size when I was born.

While everything has gone as smoothly as possible thus far we still have a lot of things that we need to take care of not the least of which is figuring out a few more options for his name. Other things that we are working on are pulling together his room, setting a delivery date, and bracing ourselves for the changes that are ahead. We will get them done I just don't know when and in what order!

2015:
SAYING HELLO AND GOODBYE!

JANUARY 6: TAKING TURNS

With everything that is going on lately with the move, work, lodge, and other things, I was looking forward to going to the next doctor appointment to check on our baby. That's right, I actually had a reason to look forward to a doctor appointment. With our scheduled checkup a little later in the evening, I left the office a little later than usual and called my wife during the commute. It has been, to say the least, a little chaotic for her lately as well and she too was looking forward to hearing our son's rapid heartbeat.

In the past we have endured prolonged periods in the waiting room so as the first flakes of precipitation brushed across our cheeks we walked into the office a little early and settled in for what we expected to be another long evening. Thankfully we were wrong as before we could even get settled, and certainly to the displeasure of those who were already waiting, we were escorted back to an examining room. Once all the basic vitals were checked, it was time for my wife to lay down and let the baby take over the moment.

As many of you know and have experienced before, hearing your child's happy heartbeat takes over the moment allowing for everything else that may be going on in your life to disappear for a brief moment. Last night it couldn't have come at a better time as that one instant, that fleeting flutter of a moment, made much of the thoughts from the previous few days, weeks, and months disappear from our thoughts. It didn't last long of course but it was enough to get us through the rest of the day and into the night.

In the end, our baby remains healthy and slightly ahead of schedule. That is really all that we want. It just happens to be a bonus that he is already starting to listen to us, sleeping when we need to sleep, and shifting into a different position when needed. Even if he didn't do any of those things we would still love him just as much as we do now and that, our new reality as parents, continues to be what is getting us both through many tough moments lately. Essentially, baby is already helping to take care of us now before we have to start taking care of him.

And now we wait for the next appointment. While we just had the most recent checkup last night, we are already looking forward to the next one. Before long he will be here and that is when our lives will really change but, for now, we are enjoying the change that he has already had on our lives.

JANUARY 11: BABY SHOWER

It was bitterly cold as I left the house on Saturday morning to get the oil changed at the dealer. My wife and I had planned on meeting up in Wayne later in the day just before her baby shower. However, as soon as I pulled into one of the service parking spots, and saw the crowd in the waiting room through the window, I knew we were going to have to adjust things. Unfortunately, I didn't realize just how much our plans would change.

My wife picked me up on her way to the late lunch and while in transit I called my dad to have him pick me up at the venue. This was my wife's day and I didn't want to stick around too long and get in the way. After chatting with a few people and greeting some early arrivals, it was time for me to head out and wait for both the call from the dealer and the text from my wife.

While we chatted about work, planning for the year, and other things the dealer finally called about 2-3 hours after I first walked through their doors. It turns out that my car needed more than just an oil change as the front brakes needed to be replaced and the slow leak that I had them check on the front tire was actually a bent rim… I guess I won't be seeing my car for a few more days. Well, things happen and thankfully my wife was having a much better day.

The shower was a small gathering of family and friends all of which brought overly generous bags and boxes. We had put a lot of things on the registry but simply to offer a variety of both items and prices thereof, we didn't expect so many items to be purchased. When I got the text from my wife, I was glad to read that things had gone well and that she was happy. Everything else didn't really matter at that moment… my wife had a good time and everything had gone as smooth as possible.

We met up at the tail end as the last guests were walking out the door. The bags and boxes seemed never ending as we walked back and forth between the restaurant and a few cars. Thankfully we had some help from my family as well as a bigger place to live in which to fit all of this new stuff. The help continued later in the evening as my sister and brother-in-law (along with the kids) helped us get everything in the house and move around the furniture that I was unable to get up the stairs previously.

It was a long and tiring day for both of us but a great day and one that will serve as a happy memory for us and many of our family members. And now we will wait for our son to arrive so that we can start using all the new items that will soon be organized in his room… which is another project all together. I guess that is going to have to be the new project.

January 25: Cursing At The Furniture

For the past several evenings I have been able to get out of the office at a normal time and head straight home without having any other obligations in the evening. There was also a few free hours the past couple of weeks. This "free" time was quickly cashed in so that we could finally get everything put together and moved into place in the baby's room. By the end of the day I was really wishing that Babies R Us had offered assembly when we ordered online.

All of the furniture arrived earlier this month and has been sitting in pieces in the middle of the room. It is not that putting together the functional jigsaw puzzles was complicated it really just came down to finding the time to read the directions and putting them together. The first attempt to do so came last Saturday when hutch pieces were strewn across the floor and I started screwing the pieces together. Ten minutes later the initial project was put on hold as the pot metal hardware bent and broke thanks to a few holes that were drilled too deep. This was only the beginning of the cursing at inanimate objects portion of the day.

After a quick trip to Home Depot for some replacements and spares, we got back on track putting things together. I built the furniture and my wife supervised… our son isn't old enough to help lift things yet. It is a model that has worked in the past so why mess with it. An hour in and the hutch was put together and attached to the dresser. I could see my wife's eyes light up as the first piece was put into place (and then put into a new place when we reconsidered the layout.

The crib and changing table was next. It is safe to say that directions are not the company's strong suit as there were numerous instances of putting together, taking apart, and reassembling parts where the instructions were clearly left to interpretation. However, with the sun slowly setting and the lamp we found on clearance prolonging the work day, everything finally came together leaving only the glider still in its box.

The glider and ottoman proved to be, by far, the easiest items to build and within 20 minutes of putting the crib in the corner, the room was complete. My wife, both tired and eager, soon followed by letting me know of her plans of where she wanted to place the pile of things that we received at the baby shower. By the time we went to bed that night, some of those things were already in place.

Now we are down to the details. Getting the clothes cleaned, organizing the shelves, decorating the walls (thanks to the clearance sections at Babies R Us), and stocking the room with many of the things that we will need for our son. It is all coming together and while many of the things are in place and ready, I am sure that there are even more things that we are forgetting about and will only remember once we need them. Until then, we will get everything else together and wait for baby.

JANUARY 29: THE TIMES THEY ARE A CHANGING...

We are now getting to the point in the pregnancy when there is nothing that can really make my wife comfortable and, therefore, there is no way that I am going to be comfortable. Sleep is sporadic at best and the smallest amount of stress (completely unavoidable at this point) causes the occasional contraction. While that may be worrisome to many, we are at the point when this is a completely normal irregular thing to happen. It's when they become regular that we have to considering hauling to the hospital.

We still have some things that we need to take care of around the house but, overall, everything seems to be under control. With that said, there seem to be things that will come about every other day that just throw all of our plans out the door (where they are stomped on and lit on fire). I guess that is just another way to prepare us for having a baby in our life... you really have to take things as they come once he arrives.

The doctor appointments are now every week with the mad rush out of the office becoming more and more difficult but still completely manageable. And so far, with the exception of a few times when we have had to wait a little longer than usual or reschedule due to weather, everything has checked out and our son is happy, healthy, and active to the point that even the nurses are surprised. The doctor actually considers our son's development completely normal... I guess he shouldn't get used to being described that way given the family around him.

It's funny that many of the conversations that I've had with people they all expect me to be nervous and 'not ready yet' but, above all else, I am excited to see and hold our son. As each day passes the anticipation grows and the nerves subside ever so slightly. I don't expect this to be easy but I am looking forward to his arrival probably more than anything else that I have waited for in my life.

I wish that was the only thing that was going on in our lives right now but nothing in life is ever easy no matter how smoothly things may seem to be progressing at times. We have to take the bad with the good no matter how hard it is to handle. With everything that surrounds us and occupies our days, I can't wait for that moment when I can hold our baby and forget about everything else that is going on in the world (even if he decides to poop on me).

February 8: Not Much Longer Now...

I really don't know where the time has gone. It feels as though we had just surprised the family only a short time ago with the announcement but it has now been eight and a half months and our son's arrival is fast approaching. On the one hand I wish that we had more time to prepare the house and ourselves but on the other hand I can't wait for the day when we can meet our baby.

The emotions have been running high lately with the stress even higher. The one constant during this time has been the comfort that our child brings when I feel him moving beneath my hand. Having him already starting to bond with me in that small way has made many days and countless moments bearable and the world just a little bit better. It is interesting to think that his arrival will make things so much more complex but at the same time simplify things like we have never experienced before.

Both of us have our moments of eagerness, times of stress, and instances of panic and nervousness. There are times when we want the birth to happen right then and there and other moments when we wish we had just a couple more weeks. With so many things that have been going on I wish we had more time to enjoy the anticipation and excitement. Those moments have been too few and far between.

Looking back there are moments that I will forever cherish... remembering the moments when decisions were made, furniture was slowly constructed, and the times when I was able to stand back for a few minutes and watch my wife fold baby clothes and put them away. I will never forget those moments that the two of us shared. They will remain prominent right there with the moments when we told our parents, the first time we saw our son and heard his heartbeat, and the even going back to the instant when we both agreed that we were ready to start a family many years ago sitting along King George Street in Jerusalem.

It has been a long time coming and while it may not have seemed like it was moving along so quickly in the moment, time has moved so fast and I wish we could just slow things down so we could enjoy the moments, minutes, and seconds. So many things have changed since that instant when we found the strength to become parents and all the trials since that discussion have continued to prepare us for what is just over two weeks away. While I still question whether I will be a good father I know that we will be a great family. Or, at the very least, an interesting one.

February 15: A Little Early

When my wife woke me up in the middle of the night saying that she still wasn't feeling well I did my best to comfort her even though I was still half asleep. Having just been to the hospital, her flu was something that needed to be watched but sometimes my wife can be a little more overzealous in her monitoring. However, even having been woken up a few times before and still suffering from a week long lack of sleep, there were a few words that my wife uttered that immediately got me up and out of bed... "I think my water just broke." That will wake you up faster than the strongest cup of coffee the world has ever known.

After another call to the doctor to let them know that we were coming in, we packed everything up, jumped in the car, and made our way back to the hospital. We were still in shock by the quick turn of events but there was an odd calm in the car despite the bitterly cold winds blowing the snow all over the roads. By 5am we pulled up to the labor and delivery entrance to Bryn Mawr Hospital. Not surprisingly, the doctor confirmed what we had suspected, what my wife had surmised an hour prior and we knew that the by the time the day ended we would have a small addition to our family.

With family already beginning to arrive, we were escorted into the operating room where I was able to peek over the curtain and see my son being born. As many of you know, when your child is first born they look like a cross between an alien and a miniature member of the blue man group but that doesn't make you think twice about wanting to reach over and hold him. At 9:14am our son, our little boy, was born and our priorities forever changed. If only the post office delivered packages this early we would never have a problem with the postal system again.

Unfortunately, since my wife was diagnosed with the flu less than 24 hours prior, we are confined to gowns and masks for the duration of our stay in the hospital. With that said, that hasn't deterred us from holding him every chance that we have had today and just looking in awe at the beautiful boy that we have brought to this world. Now the real work and the real worry begins as I hope to be a good father in addition to being a good husband. However, the second that I saw him I knew in that instant that I would do anything for him.

Happy Birthday My Beautiful Baby Boy!

February 16: Making Our Last Words Count

Last Friday, for reasons that we cannot explain, my wife and I decided to tell one person, just one, the name that we had chosen for our son. My mother-in-law, having been diagnosed with stage 4 lung cancer just before my wife's birthday in October and had not been well for some time, was the only one that we wanted to tell. And while she didn't give an acknowledgement of the news that we had shared, there is little doubt that she heard us.

Our son was the light of the day which was able to pierce the darkest of moments. Having joined the world at 9:14am we were quick to send a photo to family and friends to let them know of the joy that had just been bestowed upon us. Even my mother-in-law who had not been communicative for several days opened her eyes when she was told that a picture of her first grandchild was sent to her. For the first time in days she spoke a single word… wow!

Still in shock from the early arrival of our baby boy, my wife and I were slowly recovering from the day that had just transpired. With all visitors having left the maternity ward for the day we settled into our hospital beds and waited for our son to come back into the room for his next meal. It was at this point about 12 hours since our son entered the world that my wife made a request to the nurse… one that I am sure that they are not used to hearing.

It was a simple act but it was a moment that would immediately become part of family lore. My wife turned to the nurse and asked her to make our son cry while she had her mother's caretaker on speakerphone next to her mom's bed. The nurse didn't question my wife and seconds later his cry was echoing in my mother-in-law's great room. My wife followed by saying "I love you" and told the caretaker that she would call back in the morning. It was a call that she wouldn't have the opportunity to make.

What we didn't find out until later was that mere seconds after hearing the healthy cry of her grandson, my mother-in-law took her last breath. She held on just long enough, and our son arrived just early enough, that she was able to leave this world as a grandmother. The circle of life, in all its joy and pain, mystery and misery, beginning and ending was in full display. In a matter of half a day we were both overjoyed and heartbroken.

Since that moment, we have been experiencing the full range of emotions remembering both the good times and bad, the disagreements and the celebrations, the moments of happiness and of sadness. I have been doing all that I can to try and comfort my wife knowing that there is no real comfort that can be given during this time. Only our son can bring solace and help to heal my wife's heart and the knowledge that the last words that we both spoke to her were the most powerful and comforting things that we could ever say to her in her last moments in the physical world... our son's name and "I love you".

February 17: Tinkle Tinkle Little Star

When a new baby enters your life you are sometimes guilty of too much information when talking about some of the daily (and not so daily) occurrences of living with a newborn.

My wife and I have spent the last couple of days trying to get our heads around what has happened and all the changes in our lives. There have been times when our room seemed to have a revolving door and others when we were able to take a few breaths between the family and medical professionals walking in and out of the room. Of course there have also been a few entertaining moments in between as well.

One of the things that I am having to learn is how to change a diaper. My wife, with her previous work experience, is much more familiar with the process and a heck of a lot more efficient too. However, my skills at this point are virtually nonexistent. With that said, there have already been times when we both had to stand back and laugh at what had transpired.

A perfect example of this was earlier today when baby released a rather robust colonic announcement leaving us no alternative than to take him to his crib and see if I was improving at all in my changing abilities. While things seemed to be going much faster and I was upsetting him just a little less, it didn't take long before baby let us know that we can't expect each changing to go smoothly.

Shortly after we finished wiping everything off, with his rear high in the air, a steady rain began falling around our son. Yeah, we missed that part of the changing process. With a fresh sprinkle of tinkle across his chest and on his face, we grabbed a handful of wipes and cleaned him off again while trying our best to control the nearly crippling laughter that had resulted from the stream. Thankfully baby didn't really think twice about it and we were soon getting some new clean clothes on him. We are sure that this is only the first of many and that it will probably stop being funny in the future but this time we really needed the laugh.

February 18: Quality Time Away From The Lodge

It should be no surprise that I wasn't at the lodge last night. Instead we were still in the maternity ward with our son maintaining the annoying face mask boundary. While in the past I may have been annoyed that I wasn't there to support my brothers in their education, I was much happier supporting my wife and son as they both recovered. And while I may not have been able to spend time with my lodge brothers last night, I was able to introduce my brother to his new nephew which proved to be one of the highlights of the day.

As soon as my wife woke me up early Sunday morning I knew that my schedule (in addition to our lives) would be just a little different this week so it didn't take long before a sent a mass text to some of the usual attendees letting them know of my joyous absence. I wrote the following and sent it to about a dozen members of the lodge: "Due to the arrival of my future mason, I will be unable to attend lodge this week. Feel free to call if you need me for anything."

Since sending that message I have received a flood of support from my fellow brothers. It was one congratulatory text after another to the point that my phone seems to be getting a little tired of having to chime and vibrate so often. Family comes first is not just something that we say because it sounds good, every brother in the lodge lives by that simple saying and supports those masons who also embrace that way of thinking and living.

These immediate gestures are what I hope to share with my son when he comes of age. It is a bond, a fellowship, and a true brotherly love that cannot be matched in any other civilian organization. It is something that I hope to share with my son as he gets older and now is the time that I am building the groundwork so that he can join the fraternity with a long standing connection with the brotherhood. After all, the next generation is reliant on the current generation especially when it comes to continuing a family legacy.

I may not have much to offer my son at this point but I am going to work hard each and every day so that he will look at me the same way that I see my own father. He will know from where he comes (both my family tree as well as my wife's) and he will be able to build upon what has been achieved before him in every generation. This includes my duty as a mason and instilling in him the faith, character, and virtues that we all hold as brothers of the craft.

FEBRUARY 19: COMING HOME

When we were given the option of leaving on Wednesday or Thursday we did take a few moments to think about it. However, being confined to our hospital room since we arrived, it really wasn't a hard decision to make even with the linger fears of heading out on our own. So once the doctor came in for our morning visit, we let her know that we were ready to go and that we would be out and on the road by midafternoon.

The first part of the prep was making sure that the car seat was secured in the back of the car. I vaguely recall having done this in the past when my niece still used one (she's 20 now) but that little piece of knowledge has long since shaken out of my head. It's not a difficult process by any means but when you are trying to make sure that your child is safe every parent, no matter how laid back, gets incredibly OCD about these kinds of things.

We got the room packed up, secured our surprisingly quiet son in his car seat, and called for an escort to help us get down to the lobby and out front to our car which I had pulled up earlier. It was a surreal feeling knowing that we came to the hospital just a few days ago still as a married couple and now we were leaving as a family of three. We were about to enter the real world covered in a fresh coating of snow and a bitterly cold wind barreling down the street.

With all three of us secured in our seats and the pile of stuff crammed in the trunk, I slowly pulled around to the stop sign and started our drive home. I can't recall any other point in my life being so careful and deliberate behind the wheel… not even during my driving test. Needless to say, with a new baby and my wife still recovering from major surgery, it took a little longer than expected to get to the house but we made it there safe and sound.

Walking in the door we knew things were completely different and that coming home meant so much more now than it did in the past. We were home and ready to start living our life as a family. However, starting off, just like with the car, I am sure that we are going to have plenty of OCD and overprotective moments. Such is the beginning of parenthood.

February 22: Fulfilling The Mitzvah

Last night the snow and ice descended upon us covering everything in a frigid tapestry devoid of color. This was the landscape to which we awoke today, the perfect clean slate by which our son was to start his life as a member of the tribe. However, just like the faith that he has been born into, sometimes there are unseen trials that are cause for caution. Just outside our front door was a pristine shell of crystal clear ice. We took our time and made it out the door later than we had expected but we were safe and that is what really mattered.

After a quick stop at my parent's house to pick up some backup, we made our way into center city Philadelphia and arrived at my father-in-law's apartment about 20 minutes behind schedule. Family and friends were already packed into the place and overflowing into the hallway when we arrived and before we could make our way to the middle of the crowd the mohel (who was also the mohel for my conversion) whisked us away to the back bedroom to make sure that we (including our son) were prepared for the experience that was about to follow.

For those of you who are not familiar, the mohel is the person in the Jewish faith who performs the mitzvah of brit milah, the covenant of circumcision, which was commanded by G-d to Abraham over 3,700 years ago. While rushed to begin, the mohel took his time during the ritual and made sure that our son was brought into the covenant the way that it should be done. After all, you don't want a mohel to cut any corners.

While the act itself is something that is difficult to see, especially when it is your own son, it is also an incredibly moving moment for both the parents and the grandfathers. This is the moment that our son became a child of Israel. It was a moment that I will never forget and one that I am glad I was able to share with my family. Following the performance of this sacred mitzvah, our son was given his Hebrew name which was easy for us to decide but one that also carries great meaning.

The morning continued with our son a little sleepy and tipsy from the Manischewitz he was given before, during, and after the brit. The rest of us reveled in the glory and holiness of the mitzvah that had just taken place. Of all the moments and experiences that I have had within my chosen faith this, by far, is the one that carried with it the most meaning and made me feel closer to G-d. Our son was now a Jew just like his mommy and daddy.

FEBRUARY 24: POO RAINBOW

Not long after our son arrived and they brought him back to our room in the maternity ward we were warned of all the things that we would be encountering when we changed his diaper. "Oh, the things you'll see" as Dr. Seuss would say. However, words can't really express the interesting moments of discovery when we peeled back the tabs and saw the carnage laid upon Pooville.

It all started with the tar pit. This is the kind of nasty stuff that they find dinosaurs in and what they use to patch highways. It's like trying to clean up a pile of black superglue. I was half tempted to call the EPA when his diaper seemed as though it was attached with Velcro and the wipes seemed to whimper in the corner of the bassinet.

Slowly but surely these emanations transformed into a consistency that we are all familiar with. "Pardon me, do you have any Grey Poopon?" Why yes, yes I do. That's right, I was never a big fan of mustard to begin with but I am certainly avoiding it now that I have seen the "seedy Dejon" that our son had been producing. And that is exactly how the doctors and nurses describe the consistency… it is even found in the little take home poo packet.

Seeing all this is one thing but seeing it in action is another. Last weekend we found ourselves playing the part of Lepookans doing our best to avoid being caught at the end of the poo rainbow. Ever since we found out and told people that we were having a boy they all warned us to block the winkie but no one bothered to inform us of the other fountain that poses a threat to new parents.

We were nearly done changing his diaper and about to pull up his new Pampers when all of the sudden someone decided to squeeze the mustard bottle and my wife and I ducked for cover. Thankfully there weren't any fans in the room that it could hit and really cause a mess. Safe to say we had a little extra laundry that had to be done that night and I seriously considered putting up a splash guard at the end of the changing table.

However, even with the flurry of fierce feces, things have been going pretty smoothly and, most importantly, baby seems to be happy. He's a bit of a gassy little baby but none of that matters when I pick him up and he smiles as he looks at me. Of course, there are those interesting times when he holds his hand out seemingly saying "Daddy, pull my finger!"

routine. It was also nice to be around people, around friends, rather than being limited to conversations over the phone. But while it was great to be back it didn't take long before I was looking forward to going home and holding my son. Yes, things have changed quite a bit.

MARCH 2: RETURNING TO THE OFFICE

Before our son arrived I had sat down with some of the people at work and we put a plan together as to how many days I would be taking off and how long I would be out of the office. Well, that plan didn't fit neatly into the schedule that we all had in mind. However, the basic timeline that we had come up with worked out pretty well when the early arrival happened.

For the past week and a half I have been getting up in the morning, sitting at the kitchen table, and doing my best to get all the work done that I would normally take care of at the office. Occasionally I would step away from the computer to change the baby or go to CVS and pick up some essentials absent from our home. It may not have been the most efficient means to get work done but it was completely manageable and I was able to both spend some time with my wife and son and catch up on a few things that needed to get taken care of. The commute was pretty good too.

After two weeks away from the office, I got in my car in the early morning and drove the 40 minutes down the highway. It was both difficult to leave my family and a welcomed return to my routine. However, it didn't take long before I noticed just how different things were from the time I walked out the door in the middle of the last month. In addition to the many conversations with colleagues and requests for more pictures, I noticed a photo hanging from the office refrigerator when I walked into the kitchen to make my first cup of coffee.

I had completed the trifecta of children posted on the fridge over the past year with two of my colleagues posting pictures of their sons when they were born last year. Three men from the office had three sons… the women have a lot of catching up to do. It has almost become a tradition now to post the photos of the new additions to the work family.

Thankfully, I was able to enjoy the moments of coming back to the office after such a long time away and soon found myself getting back into my

MARCH 16: ONE FAST MONTH

It is hard to believe that a month has already passed since our son decided to surprise us. We had been planning for his anticipated arrival for many months but when he showed up we were taken off guard. Even if everything had gone according to plan I think we still would not have felt as if we were prepared. I guess that just comes with the territory.

Since that early February morning, things have been a little hectic to say the least. It has been both a challenge and a time of wonder watching him adapt to life outside of the womb. Each day there is something a little different. Sometimes it is a rather unpleasant surprise while other times there are moments of awe when my son hears me come home from work and smiles.

The nights can sometimes be long (more so for my wife) and the days go by way too fast. I don't know where the last month has gone. All the while we have done our best to adapt and get acquainted with the fact that our life is completely different and our priorities have changed significantly.

There have been moments when people have been tremendously helpful and there have been times when those people, contrary to their good intentions, have been quite the hindrance. All the while our son has been surprisingly understanding of all that is going on around him and, for the most part, has not unleashed a plethora of protesting cries. It is a steep learning curve which we sometimes struggle with but have, thus far, been able to maintain.

Now I find myself with a lot left that I still have to learn, stories that I look forward to sharing with my baby, and a schedule that still needs some tweaking. All of this tends to go out the window on a daily basis as our little boy wants nothing to do with schedules and plans. We are all trying to just take things as they come, coordinate the best we can, and see how each day and night plays out.

Of course, this doesn't mean that I can't look forward to the future so I am slowly forming my baby bucket list that began germinating not long after we found out that we were having a child. Some of the things are common events during development like hearing his first words, watching him crawl and walk for the first time, and enjoying the silence as he sleeps through the night. Other things are very specific like sharing our hobbies, our family history, and taking him to the places that we enjoy visiting.

This is just a quick overview of what I am jotting down here and there. But, for now, I am going to keep it simple and enjoy the wonders of the first month and these first memories that my wife and I have of our new life as a growing family.

MARCH 19: A GOOD PLACE TO SLEEP

When we first moved into our last place we didn't have much to fill the space and it took some time before we were able to make the small apartment comfortable. Over time we accumulated a fair amount of stuff and by the time we finally got out of that building we were able to fill much of our current house. In fact, it was nice spreading things out across multiple rooms.

Since we first hauled everything through the door it has, once again been a slow accumulation of stuff. The vast majority of these new items were not optional as we had a long list of things that our son was going to need both when he arrived and soon after. It is safe to say that this has filled the rest of the rooms and overall space that we gained when we moved here.

However, of all the things that we have accumulated lately there are a couple of items that are particularly meaningful to us as family is very important to me and my wife. This is why we were excited when my mom thoroughly cleaned and mended the family bassinet so that we could use it in our home. My grandparents bought the bassinet 75 years ago and it has been passed around the family ever since providing a bed to countless relatives.

It wasn't until after our son arrived that we were given something from my wife's side of the family with the same kind of history behind it. My wife's cousin approached us and said that she had something very special for our son. As it turns out my wife's great grandmother had knitted a blanket over 40 years ago for her cousin but, for one reason or another, it was never used. It was put away in a closet for over four decades before they decided to give it to our son.

The two are now together… two families now one. We don't hold on to many items that carry so much history but it is nice to have just a few that we can use and, more importantly, that our son can use. Now, every day, our son takes his naps surrounded by both sides of his family and over 100 years of combined history.

March 21: What's In A Name?

One of the hardest if not the hardest decision that my wife and I had to make was when we had to come up with a name for our son. We went back and forth countless times and consulted more books and websites than I can recall each time writing down anything that appealed to us. We couldn't decide between choosing a traditional Jewish name and those names that can be found in our extensive family trees. After we each wrote a few options down we would share with one another which eliminated many of the possibilities. More still were eliminated when we considered the names of some of our young relatives.

After several months going back and forth we had a few options both of first names and middle names, Jewish names and family names, some that we both really liked and others that had a certain amount of indifference with one or both of us. About a week before our son arrived we sat down and looked at the options that we both liked. We played around with the names switching between first and middle as well as family and non-family names. We also considered some of the surnames on my wife's side for the middle name... after all it has worked for me.

I guess there were about 5 first and 5 middle names that it came down to. Not being able to figure out what exactly fit our son we both took turns just saying them out load to see what sounded right. This is when we notice something very special. Each time we read the names our son decided to cast his vote. It didn't matter whose voice, he consistently kicked, punched, or head butted when we would say each name... one first and one middle. Not many parents can say that their son chose his own name but we can.

His first name is one that runs throughout both sides of my family. When looking throughout the tree I see it across many branches with various surnames in tow: Teaford, Hallman, Uttley, Redcross, Cooke, Clapsaddle, Ardis, Noblit, and a few others. It runs throughout the generations and it has always been a family name. In addition to the recent significance and honor that the name carries it was also the name of my great great grandfather Uttley, a member of the Philadelphia Police Department for over 50 years, who raised my grandmother after her parents divorced. My 5th great grandfather Redcross, member of the Monacan Nation and Revolutionary War soldier. My great grandfather Hallman who served in WWI. My 5th great grandfather Noblit, one of the early residents of Middletown Township in Delaware County who saw much of his property seized during the Revolution.

With our son selecting his first name from my side his middle name had to be one of significance in my wife's family. Thankfully our son agreed and chose a name which, according to what I have been told is the name of the last in a long line of Rabbis on my wife's side. My wife's great grandfather Greenburg may have passed nearly a decade before she was born but his legacy still lives to this day. Born in Romania and having come to the United States around the turn of the 20th century as a child, he supported his family the best he could and raised my wife's grandmother whom she still misses. In the end, our son chose names from the men who raised both of our grandmothers to which we were very close. He also made picking a Hebrew name really easy.

Some hear it and wonder how we came up with the name, which we have been asked many times over, and while we did consider the origins of the names (which did seem to fit our son), the family meaning behind them is far more significant. While we have both given the short answer during the course of conversations, this is the full story behind his name. Our son has a part of each of us, myself and my wife, but more importantly he carries with him a long family history on both sides of which he can be proud and all he has to do to remember that is look at his own name.

MARCH 22: THE HARDEST PART

There have been many difficult moments during these early days of parenthood with the hardest of which happening today. Last night I couldn't sleep as I didn't want today to come. I knew that when I woke up the morning would go too fast and my departure would arrive too soon. This morning I woke up knowing that I would have to leave my family for a few days while I traveled to Chicago for work.

The plane was scheduled to depart just after lunch so we all piled in the car around 9:30 so that there wouldn't be any timing issues. With my wife behind the wheel I sat beside my son staring at him as the mile markers streamed by the window. It was a ride that seemed to go on forever and one that ended way too soon.

While he usually sleeps whenever he is in the car, this time was different. He kept opening his eyes and looking at me as if to catch one last glimpse before daddy had to leave. Each time this happened was just as hard as the last.

When we arrived I moved slowly to prolong the moment. I kissed my son and kissed my wife. Then I watched them drive away as I made my way to the terminal doors.

Even with the cluster at the counter when I found out US Airways and American Airlines aren't talking anymore, the confusion at security where there were no signs directing which line to get in, and the debacle at the gate when seat assignments were handed out to all passengers, I still kept thinking about the looks from my son each time he woke up in the car. It is a look that persisted in my mind throughout the day. Even later in the night during the client meeting and, after that, spending time with a friend that I haven't seen in over 3 years, I was still thinking about my wife and my son.

It is interesting to think about the changes that have occurred since the last time that I was on a business trip like this. Last year this whole thing was still new having only been at the company for 6 months, it was just my wife and me, and business travel was something with which I was still unfamiliar. While by no means old hat, it is just a different experience this year. Same company, similar trip, a new son, and reconnecting with an old friend.

Things are different this year. It is going to be a great trip and an excellent event but I know my thoughts will remain with my family. Three nights until I can see my wife and son again. Until then, I have to work and enjoy the pictures that my wife will certainly be sending me. Those are the moments to look forward to each day.

MARCH 26: BACK TO THE OFFICE (EVENTUALLY)

While the worst part about traveling for business is being away from my family, running in a close second is the pile of work that needs to be done once I get back to the office. It really doesn't matter if it is a day or a week, there is going to be a mountain of things that need to be taken care of once you walk into work. This is also true when taking time off but to a much lesser extent... I have been working all week but there are still things that I have yet to get done.

Of course, it didn't help this morning that I was working from home. We had rescheduled our son's doctor appointment for later in the morning and I wanted to make sure that I was present for the checkup. We had originally scheduled the visit for 10:50. A few days ago it was bumped up to 10:40 which I wasn't complaining about. So we arrived right on time (it helps that the office is only a couple blocks away) and we waited. This was followed by more waiting. An additional wait ensued after that until we were finally brought back to the examining room about 45 or 50 minutes after our scheduled appointment time.

Everything went well and our baby boy is growing and healthy but not happy after another shot and being stuck at the doctor's office for over an hour. I should mention that throughout this whole morning, including the time in the waiting room, I was fielding calls from work and lodge trying to keep everyone calm and projects moving along as scheduled. As soon as we got home I had to immediately grab my work bag, turn around, and head to the office.

It was nice getting back on the road and at my desk for the rest of the day. That feeling lasted about as long as it took to get my computer back up and running and seeing all the emails updating to my account. I had seen the number of correspondences from my phone but now I took a closer look and saw that they all required my attention and were not just CC's or updates that I can put off for a little while. A long afternoon followed a long morning but, thankfully, many of the things that I had been dreading seeing on my desk never showed up. I am still trying to catch up and probably will throughout the weekend but there was good progress made despite the chaos and delays of the day.

MARCH 30: A FAMILY OF THREE

Sometimes the easiest and hardest thing you can do is to ask someone for help. This is especially true when you have your first child. While there was a part of us that just wanted to do it ourselves, we knew that with everything that was going on around us it would, at the very least, be a difficult undertaking. It is with this in mind that we decided to have a doula (also known as baby nurse or postpartum nurse) assist us during the first month.

We first met one of the doulas when we were still in the hospital trying to center ourselves again after all that had transpired over the first 24 hours as a family. With our son arriving a little earlier than expected, there were a number of projects around the house that we had yet to complete. This is when we experienced one of the big perks of having this extra help as I was able to take her to the house and show her a few of the things that we would like taken care of before we got home (mostly laundry, dishes, and a few organization projects).

When we opened the door, there were a number of things checked off our list. Maybe the most important one was that we were able to go to bed that night and sleep on clean sheets. This support continued for the next several weeks as we became more comfortable with having a newborn in our life and while we had to deal with a variety of other events beyond our control.

As time passed, the help continued to be appreciated (most recently while I was on my annual business trip) but the need to be alone with our son continued to grow. Our routine was taking shape and we looked forward more and more to the times when it was just the three of us. It was time to do things on our own and look to family and friends for the advice we needed from time to time (we still sought the advice before but now it is what we solely rely upon when needed).

We still question whether we held on to the doula safety net too long but, in hindsight, we know that there were moments early on when it would have been a struggle without their presence. But now we have our routine and our son expects to see us rather than someone else when he gets fussy or wakes up in the middle of the night. While the constant support may be good for some for a long period of time, it is not something that we wanted to last and now we can enjoy life as a family of three.

MARCH 31: FEED ME!

Every once in a while our son can be rather fussy. During those moments he can cry for a myriad of reasons but usually it revolves around food. Sometimes he is hungry while other times he is just tired. He is an odd little monkey.

Watching my wife feed our child is something beautiful to see. Those of you who have children know what I am talking about. However, there are some moments of humor during those moments that don't take away from the experience they just add some color to the process. This is even more pronounced when someone other than his mom tries to feed him.

Regardless of who is feeding him the expressions on his face are an interesting study. I'm sure he would fit right in at the Actor's Studio. Sometimes it can be a subtle smirk while other times it is a slight crinkle as he shifts and stretches. And, of course, there are the red faced moments when you know that an eruption is about to happen.

That is the other part... the sound effects. There is a certain amount of squeaking, grunting, and occasional burping that takes place (usually while his arms and/or legs are going) which is to be expected. There are also the times when he decides to try and communicate by stringing together those grunts and squeaks while gesturing. And, let's not forget the aforementioned explosions that add a certain punctuation to the process. Let's just say that our child is rather advanced in this area.

When someone else besides his mom tries to feed him there are a few other things that happen. First, he will give you the look of "what the heck are you doing?" This is followed by a quick look around for his mommy and sometimes a squint and split second cry just before the bottle is put in his mouth. Sometimes he fights the feeding while other times his hunger just takes over. But once he starts, it is pretty much the same regardless of who is feeding him at this point. However, he does seem to enjoy seeing the reaction on faces when he blasts one... mommy has gotten pretty used to it after all.

So the feeding time with baby can be interesting but mostly it is entertaining. This is especially true when he gives you a surprised look of "that came out of me?" after he lets go of a good burp or fart. That is probably a look that I will always remember. Funny how the more "interesting" moments and expressions stick with you.

APRIL 2: WELL, THAT WAS USELESS!

The learning curve is steep when you have your first child and there are many instances when you are scrambling to find the answers to questions that seemingly pop out of nowhere. Sometimes you reach out to family and friends who have kids to see what advice they have and chose from one of the many options that have inevitably been offered. Other times you reach out to the professionals and either call the doctor or, as we did a number of times early on, ask the doula. Each time we listen to the advice from those people who have "been there, done that."

Thanks to social media, we can get a plethora of opinions and answers to our questions in a very short amount of time. At least that is what I have seen on my wife's Facebook feed as I have usually just picked up the phone or asked someone in person when I run into them. While my approach may take longer and seem outdated by many, it is how I prefer getting the answers and advice that we need. It also eliminates the "other opinions".

I have had countless conversations and have heard the many humorous anecdotes from family and friends who used social media (mostly Twitter and Facebook; these aren't LinkedIn conversations) when they first became parents. While they received the helpful hints, tips, advice, and answers that they were looking for they also got the opinions of those who don't have kids but "read somewhere that this is the best thing to do" or passed along the half of the conversation that they heard 5 years ago when their friend was considering having a child. Basically, useless information… I actually heard of someone saying that you should hold your newborn upside down and lightly shake them if they get hiccups. Wow, just wow. Either they don't have kids or they're in jail.

While I have an opinion on just about everything there are certain things that I will not offer second hand advice on which includes parenting. And I still hold fast to that as we are only 6 weeks in so I can't really speak from experience on anything. If specifically asked, either by phone or in person, I will gladly share my experience but I can't give advice especially when there are general posts made on social media. Maybe after we have done this more than once I might offer my opinion but I doubt it.

APRIL 6: MEMORIES TO CARRY ME THROUGH MONDAY

It was a long weekend and I really wasn't looking forward to heading into the office this morning. For the last three days we were out at one place or another trying to get things done and complete some final tasks. It would have been tiring had everything gone to plan but ended up being exhausting. There were highs and lows with our son doing his best to go along with everything. While he was a bit fussy and overwhelmed, we couldn't have expected him to handle things much better than he did. With that said, we really don't want to put him through another weekend like we just had.

When I got up this morning it felt like I hadn't slept in days. While my eyes may have been closed and my body immobile, there seemed to have been little recuperation. My body was certainly sore and my head ached. And even though my gassy son was drowning out my alarm clock, it was still a sound that was more welcoming than the chirp and screech emanating from my cell phone.

Even half cognizant of all that was going on around me, I still had those few moments from the past few days that carried me through the morning hours. Seeing my son being held by his cousins is something that has been a bit overdue but happened at just the right time. While they didn't seem quite sure what to do when my wife placed him in their arms, their faces lit up and seared their reaction in my memory.

Last night also proved to be a great ending to the long (but too short) weekend as my son insisted on cooing at me as the paint peeling smell emanated from his diaper. It was the first time that we heard him make those sounds and they made me want to call out of work this morning just so I could hear them again. Obviously, I will have to make do with the memory which carried me through my commute this morning.

While on that drive my wife called me not long after I got on the highway. I was anticipating less than good news, when I picked up the phone I could hear the understated excitement in her voice. Our son wasn't just cooing, he was laughing. Even though I wasn't there to hear it for the first time I am glad that my wife was able to have that 'first experience' and now I have something to look forward to, something to carry me through the long Monday.

April 7: That Wasn't A Fart!

There are times early in the evening when there is loud rumble coming from the baby monitor. It's not so much surprising as it is impressive given the fact that our son only recently surpassed the ten pound mark. While some might be a little taken back and somewhat disgusted by these emanations the fact of the matter is that they are downright hilarious.

Usually before an eruption our son begins to squirm and make the occasional noise boarding on a cry. When this happens I turn the video on just to check in on him only to see two feet pointing straight up in the air, stomach tensed, and face scrunched. As soon as he unleashes the "Cracken", his body relaxes and he goes back to sleep.

Of course, then there are the other times when our son stops whatever he is doing (which isn't much at this point) and starts grunting and pushing to the point that his face becomes a deep red. At this point it is best to take cover. While most of the time it is nothing but air followed by a smirk there have been quite a few moments when the shrapnel tries blowing through whatever barrier stands in its way. While that part may not be funny the look of disbelief, shock, and relief on our son's face makes us laugh every time.

And when I say blow through barriers I mean blow through barriers. While I am certain that our son could fit into a smaller diaper, his colon wants nothing to do with those limited boundaries. We have been forced to move up a couple of sizes already not because of things being too tight but because the diapers failed the containment test (aka the blowout test). That is probably the most pleasant way of describing the scene when you pick up your child in the morning only to find that he has painted his back up to his shoulder blades. Not a pleasant way to wake up but one of those times when you find yourself laughing all the way to the bathtub.

While the sound effects started early on (before we left the hospital), they have only grown over time in both potency and decibel level. However, there is a bright side to this whole explosive situation. We have now gotten to the point when I can sleep through the night knowing that I have plausible deniability when I wake up. He still has a long way to go but he is proving to be a quick study.

APRIL 14: WATCH THE WINKIE!

It is pretty much guaranteed that when I get home after work our son's diaper is going to be a little bloated. At nearly 12 pounds, he doesn't really hold anything back. However, most of the time it is not what you usually think of when you hear about the droopiness of his drawers. While sometimes it is of a stinky nature, most of the time it is the flood waters that are testing the limits of the dam. This is confirmed by the bright blue racing stripe that appears on the front of the diaper.

Of course, whenever in doubt just wait for the crying to begin… our son is not a fan of the squishiness. These are the easy diapers to change… most of the time. Regardless of what he just finished doing, whenever the seal is broken and the emanations are exposed, the shields have to go up… there is just enough held back that a launch could occur at any moment.

While the nerves don't take kindly to the free flowing of flatus, it is the tinkle that usually causes the most trouble. At least with a number two you can hear him pushing and watch as his face turns a deeper and deeper shade of red. When it comes to the whiz his only tell is when his winkie decides to imitate a cold war missile drill. The launch could happen or it might not. Best thing to do is prepare the defenses and hope for the best.

My wife and I have discovered that you can really change a diaper quickly when under the threat of attack and most of the time the new diaper is on before the rain begins to fall. When this happens we just hope not to hear thunder which pretty much guarantees that precipitation is eminent. That is when we see the redness disappear and the smirk slowly grow into a full smile… at least it tames the fussiness for a moment.

In hindsight, all of this is a simple source of amusement. Thankfully, we haven't had any major issues with changing our son… not like the rainbows that we encountered during our first month. With that said, we still have to remain cognizant of the limits of the diaper sizes. Our son is growing quickly and so are his volume requirements so we are continuously aware of the issue of proper containment. Hopefully we can continue limiting the onesie casualties, stay ahead of the growth curve, and make sure we keep changing him as fast as possible.

April 16: Looking Back On The Last 2 Months

It is hard to believe that it has already been two months (and a day) since our son was born. There have been a lot of changes that have occurred, both for better and worse, with each of them bringing us to this point, two months later. While there is still a little disbelief in our eyes when we watch him sleep, my wife and I are enjoying this new phase in our life (even if we don't readily admit it when our baby is screaming in the middle of the night).

The memories are still so vivid going all the way back to the moment when we found out about our pending arrival. Each and every moment we will carry with us: the reactions when we told our parents, the first time we saw him on the ultrasound, the first time he breathed the same air as us, and all the details surrounding each of those moments and days. We will never forget them.

All of the tiring and trying moments seem to have faded leaving just those moments that remain seared into our memory: his first smile, the first time he found his thumb, the first time that he cooed at us, the first time he rolled over, his first car ride, and countless other moments. These are the times when I don't need a picture to see his smile and I don't need a recording to hear his coo. They are forever carried with us so that we can look back at the cuteness when he gets older.

It hasn't been an easy couple of months but seeing him grow and slowly become more aware of his surroundings is something that I can't really describe… all the parents reading this know what I am talking about. And the love that you have for your child is something that remains indescribable as well. There are already so many great moments and memories to look back on and so many things that we are looking forward to. Before we know it, they will all be memories.

While time has flown as our baby had grown, we remember each time he grew just a little bit. Now he is nearly 12 pounds and will soon be too big for the bassinette. It will be another interesting adjustment for us not having him beside the bed. But it is also going to be another memory to look back on… the look of a peaceful sleep that occurs when he doesn't have to listen to daddy snoring on the other side of the room.

APRIL 18: FREQUENT ERRANDS

One thing that has definitely increased both since we found out about our son's arrival and since his birth is the number of errands that we have to run. This is pretty much on a daily basis as there is always one thing or another that we have to pick up, drop off, exchange, or just get more information as well as a plethora of appointments. And it really doesn't matter how well prepared you think you are, there is always that one essential item that is missing from your stockpile of baby stuff.

I do my best to take care of most of these things, so long as they can wait until the end of the work day when I am on my way home, but, for the most part, my wife is the one that has to run back and forth trying to get everything done during the day. This would be hectic enough if it was just her but adding the preparation and logistics needed to get the baby ready and out the door adds to both the length of the commitment and the energy it takes to get some of these seemingly simple things done. I don't know where she finds the energy but, somehow, she is managing to get all of the constant errands done.

All of these small time and energy consuming trips during the day are something that we tried to prepare for but, in the end, we weren't expecting. While no one thing in particular is consuming the hours in our days, all of these small trips have added up. Some days more than others and overall having a huge impact on our schedules. Hopefully things will calm down a bit in the coming months but we are definitely not holding our breaths for that.

This is why I have been trying to stick to a more consistent schedule at work. In the past, my departure from the office has been fairly open ended. There were some nights when I would get back home well past eight and sometimes long after 10. Now I am doing my best to get home by 7 while trying to walk through the door around 6:30. This allows me to both get some of those other things done but also allows me to spend more time with our son while giving my wife a much needed break at the end of her day.

It is not a perfect system by any means but it is working fairly well thus far. It may be time to take a day off here and there to better prepare above and beyond our anticipated needs. Until then we will have to keep trying to become more and more efficient with these small trips.

April 21: Throwing Up (And Down)

Well, this is one of those inevitable things that we expected to encounter with our son. In fact, we were anticipating that this would happen more often than we are currently seeing. With that said, the throwing up is still something that happens and sometimes it is at some pretty interesting times.

Usually, the spew flows after a feeding but it is not always the case. These are the moments when he is usually half asleep and it just kind of bubbles to the surface... like in the opening credits of the Beverly Hillbillies. These are the moments that happen before we have a chance to burp him and when you just grab a wipe and make sure you get it all off of his face and neck.

Of course, there are also the occasions when there is a little more force behind the projectile. Most of the time this is when my wife picks him up just after his feeding and during the transition she gets a little shower on her shirt. For some reason my wife can deal with the poop and pee but the puke takes her back a bit. When home, I am frequently reaching for a wipe at this point.

When it comes to burping this is one of the reasons why I prefer to put him on my knee. Having him slightly bent over makes it much easier to clean up when the regurgitation occurs with only a small bit on the hand and around his mouth requiring some attention. Anything more and the floor takes the brunt of the punishment. I would rather him throw down than throw up.

In addition to the feeding related emanations, there are also the times when, for one reason or another, our son gets a little too excited or worked up and the fountain is turned on. There are times when he cries and this is a little exclamation point and there are also instances when the opposite happens and the milk streams through a wide smile. And there are some moments when what little remaining burp bubble carries some luggage with it hours after eating.

All of these moments are pretty minor even during some of the moments when there is greater volume and force than usual. They are moments that can quickly be addressed and, as was stated before, come with the daily baby routine. Of course, just like we will encounter on the other end, we are still not looking forward to the escalation that happens with the introduction of other foods.

April 28: Squishy Doesn't Mean Comfy!

Every night I look forward to crawling into bed onto the slightly squishy mattress and enjoying the comfort for a few minutes before falling asleep. Even when away from home, the same basic routine applies and while I prefer the firmer memory foam at home the plush squishiness on the road is sometimes a welcomed change. Regardless of where I am, it is this little moment of relaxation that ensures a long and restful slumber.

Our son has pretty much the same routine as his daddy. However, there is such a thing as too squishy which he proved early on within the first month of being home. It is this experience which has impacted the way that he has slept ever since.

It all started in mid-March when we heard his intense cry piercing through a rather pungent odor. It was clear that the mess in his diaper was not conducive to his ability to sleep which by this time was usually 5 or more hours at a time. When he was brought over to the changing table we couldn't really blame him for being uncomfortable. Baby's first night of swamp butt has stuck with him.

Since that night our son has, for the most part, refused to poo while he is asleep at night. Naps seem to be a big exception to the rule. Basically, our son just doesn't like the feeling of laying in his own stinky squishiness and would rather hold it in until morning.

This brings about an obvious drawback because the morning can be a rather vicious time of day. It is when everything seems to wake up and in the midst of his morning stretch everything is let loose. The people at Folgers didn't take this into account when considering what might be the most dominant smell to perfume the morning.

Unfortunately, we have also found that while he still doesn't like the feeling, he doesn't quite have the mastery of his bowels when sitting in the car seat. Those seem to be the most interesting occurrences which usually result in the changing of outfits and a strong urge to give him a quick bath. All the while, pooping is fair game when someone is holding him.

While it smells, it's messy, and it can be annoying when it happens in a newly sealed diaper, you can't help but laugh when he gives you that cheeky little smirk that he has already managed to master. He may crap, and crap a lot, but he is so darn cute while doing it that it doesn't seem that bad... at least in hind sight. And the loud loads are just funny.

MAY 5: BABY NEEDS SPACE

As the days and weeks have passed, our son keeps getting bigger and bigger. This seems to be happening way too fast (we were warned that this would happen). While he has yet to reach the 3 month mark he has already grown out of most cloths that bear that same marking and is now well into the 3-6 month items that fill his dresser.

While he is a bit chunky like his daddy, much of this outgrowth is because of his length. Because of this the swaddles that he once seemed to swim in are now too short to accommodate his outstretched legs and the bassinet that has remained beside our bed can barely contain him. His rapid growth forced us to make the switch over the weekend finally moving him out of our bedroom and into his crib in his own room.

So far he seems to like the privacy and I can't say I blame him. While he can still hear much of what is going on in the house, he no longer has to hear the snores echoing off the walls (although this amazingly didn't seem to bother him before). He has his own space in his own room… it really is amazing how fast things seem to be changing.

We have watched him slowly take over more and more of the bassinet over the last couple of months and now that he is in his crib it seems as though we have hit the reset button. It is a large crib and our growing boy seems lost in there. Thankfully, the transition was harder on my wife than our son as he is enjoying the extra room and the slightly softer sleeping surface. I guess we will now get to watch him slowly take over and outgrow his new bed.

I must admit that I do miss hearing him sleep on the other side of the room. I enjoyed the brief time when I could just lay in bed and listen for his muffled snores (and sometimes little farts). It was nice knowing that he was right there. Although it is much easier for me when I come to bed as I don't have to worry as much about waking him up. He is already growing so fast and now he has his own bedroom and his own crib (where he takes advantage of the extra space by spreading out when he is not swaddled) with his mommy still watching him on the monitor from her side of the bed. Some things just aren't going to change.

May 10: First Mother's Day

My wife and I have both been looking forward to today and dreading it at the same time. There has been a lot that has happened since the last time that the calendar noted this holiday. There is a lot that we have to celebrate and a lot that we are missing on this day. To my wife's credit, which says a lot about her strength, she decided to focus on the joy of the day and I did my best to make that a reality (even in the face of a few trying moments). Like many things these days, time is moving both fast and slow. It seemed to take forever for this day to come but it also caught us a little off guard.

For the past couple of months we had been anticipating the good and bad of the day. In an effort to focus on the former we decided to get away for a couple of days. I nearly dropped the ball on this one but managed to make it happen by booking a room early last week at Hershey Lodge. It was also late in the week when I was finally able to order flowers for my mom (for which we got a call when they were delivered yesterday)... ProFlowers.com kind of saved me on that one. We both owe a lot to our mom's and now that we have a son we understand even more the importance of this day.

We were a little apprehensive about the overnight stay at a hotel with the baby given that this was his first night away from home but, in the end, the entire trip went better than we could have ever hoped. There wasn't a single moment of crying for much of the getaway and he seemed to be happy to explore a new place and simply spend time with his mommy and daddy. Of course, it could be that maybe our son is already learning that you don't mess with mommy on Mother's Day.

While we did our best to think of all the good things that have happened and the fact that it is the first Mother's Day that we have celebrated with our son, I couldn't help but think about the one thing that I couldn't give my wife today. I didn't buy a card or flowers as there wasn't really anything that I could find that made sense... at least not this year. I could have bought a "First Mother's Day" card but it was also a first for another reason... one that I couldn't change. It was a hard day but a great day as well. I just wish that I could have given her the gift that she really wanted today.

MAY 18: THREE MONTHS!

It seems like I just posted the two month blog yesterday but here we are just over three months since our son was born (three months and three days to be exact). There have been good times and hard times throughout the last month as our son has become aware of more and more of the world around him. He is slowly learning little pieces here and there and now communicates in his own way with us (especially when daddy comes home from work). That moment when he turns his head and smiles at me is, by far, the highlight of my day.

Everyone said that these days go by fast and while there are certainly times when time seems to move very slowly, I really don't know where the last three months have gone. It is a blur of work and baby with a few memories from lodge meetings and other events. Everything seems to have faded into unimportance while the specific moments of seeing my son do things, see things, react certain ways, and sooth us remain vivid in my mind. Even some of the unpleasantries that have been experienced are quarantined into the recesses of memory. It is a hard thing to explain but many of you know exactly what I am talking about.

There are times when I have come through the door after a particularly long day at the office and everything seems to just fade away. Other times I have come home later than usual knowing I have to get some more unavoidable work done but lacking the energy to do so... sneaking up to his crib and watching him sleep is all I need to keep going and keep working that night. And when I am at work and my mind begins to drift, I think about my son and I get back on task knowing that if I don't finish things up during the week, I am going to have to spend some time away from him on the weekend tethered to my computer... I have managed to avoid working on the weekend for some time now.

It has been an interesting and quick adventure so far. There has been a lot of poop and a lot of laughs, many headaches and numerous giggles, a few hard days and countless beautiful moments. All the while we have watched him grow still not quite believing that he is here and that we are a family of three. Things have changed so much and as he understands a little bit more of the world around him we are eager to introduce him to new places and experiences and that is exactly what we have planned for the next three months.

May 19: Adjusting And Replacing

Our son is growing. This is far from a surprise but that doesn't mean that the rapidity of his growth is something that we were necessarily prepared for. We knew that we would be changing clothing sizes on a regular basis according to months but we are quickly finding out that those numbers on the back of the clothes are merely a suggestion (diapers too). Currently our three month old son is fitting comfortably in six month clothes. What can I say, we have a long baby… and a heavy baby too.

In addition to the bassinet that we previously moved him out of because of space limitations, we are now finding ourselves having to purchase a separate changing table for the same reason. We originally decided to purchase the changing table attachment for the crib that we selected. The thought that this would last a bit longer than it has was obviously a mistake. He is now only an inch away from the top and bottom which usually leads us to change him diagonally. We knew he was growing but we thought we had some more time. Looks like another visit to Amazon.

We have also been frequently adjusting his car seat. When we first started driving him around we got an insert to keep his head up and to just make things more comfortable for him. The insert is now gone and we have now had to adjust the straps twice so that he fits. All because he is getting to long for the previous setting. Again, we thought we had a little more time but that is simply not the case… time is flying and our son is growing way ahead of schedule. We wish we could slow things down and enjoy more of the moments and him as a certain size but that is one of the many things beyond our control in this adventure in parenting.

While we should probably start trying to plan for the continued growth of our, not so little, baby it seems as though any timeframe that is suggested as the 'norm' just doesn't apply. He is growing faster than all of the books, websites, and the doctors originally thought and he is slowly becoming more aware of everything around him. In nearly all categories, he is ahead of schedule regarding all means of growth. His coordination is progressing, his strength is dramatically improving, and his size is beyond what we expected. We have a healthy baby boy and that is all we could have ever hoped for.

JUNE 1: BABY BUCKET LIST

As the days fly by and our son keeps getting bigger and bigger, the list of things that I want to do with him keeps getting longer. Actually, it is not just about things I want to do with him, it is also about the milestones that I am looking forward to witnessing. While by no means my complete list of scribbles, here are a few of the things that I am looking forward to as our son grows up:

1. **First Words** – He is already proving to be quite the vocal child and while he is already making a sound similar to that of saying 'Hi' when I come home from work, I am looking forward to hearing that first distinct word. I am hoping that it will be either mommy or daddy (or something similar) but I am not completely ruling out the possibility that we could have a similar instance than that seen in "Meet The Fockers".

2. **Crawling./ Walking** – He has surprised us at this point by standing with little help from either of us (we are mostly there for stability) but he also has no interest in laying on his tummy so I am curious to see how this progresses. While a whole new host of issues arise once he becomes mobile, I am looking forward to the day when he demonstrates this little kernel of independence.

3. **Pool / Swimming** – This one is more for my wife. We haven't taken him to a pool yet. This should be an interesting experience. Hopefully he likes the pool as much as he enjoys his bath (at least the first half of the bath).

4. **Baseball** – Now we are progressing a little further in his development. While he has already shown an interest in throwing things and watching baseball on TV (made for a quiet dinner at Fox & Hound last week), I am looking forward to putting those two things together. I just hope he got his grandfather's athletic ability because it definitely skipped me.

5. **Lodge Events** – While we have taken him to the lodge once I am looking forward to the future events both at my lodge as well as other masonic events in the area (and outside the area like our trip to Pittsburgh coming up). There are a lot of us with young kids and I really want to see all of us get together for an experience far different from those on meeting nights.

6. **Synagogue** – We are a little behind on this one. While there isn't much that he will comprehend early on, we want our son to be used to going to synagogue and make it part of his routine. We need to get moving on this search.

7. **First Day of School** – Again, looking into the future. This is a milestone that I think every parent looks forward to happening. I will be there the day that this happens (mixed emotions and all). Hopefully he proves to be a better student than his father.

8. **Family History** – My wife and I have spent a lot of time learning about our families and we want to share those histories with our son. We want to make sure that he knows where he comes from and learns all about the people we come from both more recent and in the distant past. Hopefully, I can find some answers along the way and share these discoveries with him. After all, he is a continuation of both our families.

9. **Family Reunions** – This is something that my wife and I agreed is incredibly important for us as a family. We are starting this year with my side of the family (I will be writing extensively about our trip to Virginia this summer) followed by my wife's family next year. We plan on going back and forth every year. Again, we want our son to know his family and family history.

10. **Family Vacations** – In addition to bringing our son to some of the places that my wife have been and enjoyed over the last several years both local (i.e. Jim Thorpe, Gettysburg, Knoebels, etc.) and not so local (i.e. Florida, Massachusetts, London, Israel, etc.), we are also looking forward to exploring new places and destinations

with him. While we have no idea where those places will be at this point, it is still fun to think of the possibilities.

As I previously mentioned, there are countless other things that I am looking forward to but this at least gives you an idea of some of the things that I am eagerly anticipating. There are a few things that I have already been able to check off (cooing, smiling, first weekend trip, etc.) but the list is growing much faster than we are able to take things off. I guess this is also a part of parenthood… the annoying, slightly OCD, impatient part.

June 2: Blasting The Baby Monitor

When we first starting putting the baby registry together last year one of the things that we made sure to put on there was a monitor. Rather than going with the usual ones, we wanted to upgrade a little bit and get the video monitor for no other reason than we felt more comfortable being able to see our son and not just hear him. So far, that has been the primary use of the camera (especially when he is eerily quiet in his sleep) but it has also been a great source of entertainment at times.

There have been many nights when our son has had trouble sleeping or getting to sleep. Being able to see him has allowed us to take preemptive action during those times. While he may not be screaming yet, we know the restlessness that comes before the ear piercing. We both hate to hear our son cry and preventing that from happening by calming his flailing legs has been a great way to avoid those moments.

Sometimes there are moments, especially after a long and/or tiring day, when we just want to see him. It is calming to watch our son sleep but sometimes we don't want to risk stepping on that one squeaking floorboard and waking him up. The camera has afforded us the best of both worlds by watching him dreaming peacefully without the risk of disturbing those restful moments for him.

And then there are the entertaining times. Whenever we hear him rustling in his crib we turn on the video. Sometimes, as mentioned above, we need to climb up the stairs and settle him. Other times we know what is about to happen. It can be just as loud as those aforementioned screams and they are much stinker as well. Those are the times when we know he is about to let his colon calm him.

It usually starts with the legs high in the air as if he is practicing some odd form of flatulent yoga. Keep in mind that we are watching this from the foot of the crib (maybe the funniest of all the possible angles). This is followed by a little shimmy. This can happen several times depending on the intensity of the end result. Once everything is primed the fuse is lit and the explosion vibrates the crib. I guess you could say that it is a brief moment of satisfying wakefulness for our baby. Once the dust settles he turns his head to the side and falls right back into a deep and restful sleep. At this point we just hope our laughing isn't so loud that it will wake him up.

So there are many uses that we have gotten out of the video monitor. Some are very practical and have been beneficial since we brought our son home in the winter. Of course, there are also the other times when it has just been a great source of laughter.

JUNE 9: AT LEAST
IT HASN'T HIT THE FAN

Ever since we brought our son home from the hospital he has been pretty consistent at not doing one thing in his sleep… pooping. Of course, while there hasn't been any mess there has been a fairly large amount of auditory pollution but that is a topic that I have already covered. But the simple, and kind of amazing, fact is that our son learned early on that it is not comfortable to sleep in your own poo. With that said, he does not abide by a rather famous saying… he does crap where he eats.

The eruption usually occurs late in the morning or early in the afternoon. The one commonality is that it happens either during or immediately after he has his bottle. Until recently there was little doubt when this happened at the colonic alarm would usually sound. However, recently our son has employed the sniper crap… you don't realize what has happened until it is too late.

Because of these sneak attacks, there have been many casualties along the way. It is common for our son, like many babies his age, to wear a multitude of outfits during the day. While we have gotten pretty used to this routine there are occasions when we just have to take a step back, take a deep breath (not through our noses), and proceed with the usual hazmat procedures. Pretty astounding considering he is already wearing size four diapers.

And it never fails that the worst of these atomic tests occur outside of the house. Sometimes in the car and other times while we are eating in a restaurant (among other locations). Always concluding with a mischievous smirk. The latest occurred while having lunch on Saturday before we headed out looking for a new car. It was bad… it was the first time that we had to really clean the car seat.

In the end, his development and early habits are different than we could have ever anticipated. He is so far beyond where we ever expected him to be and I am excited to see how fast he continues to pick things up.

Hopefully, this is a foreshadowing for an easy potty training but I am really not counting on that one. Until then we will just have to continue our vigilance when we sit down at a restaurant and hope that wind doesn't carry the fall out across the dining room.

June 15: How Is Time Moving So Fast?

It has been an amazing month watching our son learn new things, grow, and begin to understand more of the world around him. There have been a few instances that have tested our patience especially with regard to the reflux but, overall, we couldn't have asked for a happier or loving baby. And seeing him in the morning and when I get home at night are what really completes my day. Seeing that smile on his face when I walk in the door, seemingly saying "hi daddy", never gets old and lets me forget about anything that may have been bothering me during the day.

While he is not yet found any interest in rolling over (or being on his belly for that matter), he is still doing things that are still amazing when I think about the fact that he is only 4 months old today. In addition to his enjoyment of being on his feet with little support from mommy or daddy, he also just started sitting up by himself. They may only be for a few seconds at a time but it is much more than many babies his age.

He has found a new interest in the various toys that have been sent to us or that we have picked up over the past few months. While he still prefers his ball which we have tethered to his car seat, he is also enjoying the car keys and some of the other things that we have bought. Unfortunately, he has also figured out how to throw things. He also enjoys pushing the buttons on mommy's cell phone when she is talking to daddy. The big toys are proving to be very useful as well as we can now put him in the exersaucer where he is perfectly content playing with everything around him and making the train go around the track.

While I have had to tell him for months whether or not I would be home late in the evening, he is now responding to more and more of what we are saying. He knows his name (he will learn the importance of his name later) and is able to respond to some of the simple requests that we make like to hold on when we pick him up. He is now a fully interactive child (not like the creepy one in A.I.) with each day more interesting than the last.

I am sure that I have forgotten a variety of things that have happened and developments that have occurred over the past month but that should give you a basic idea. It is quite the ride that we are on and one that keeps getting better with every dip and turn. And even though there is a lot of puking and crapping of pants, it is still a ride that we are so glad and thankful that we got on. Happy 4 months baby!

PS – Sorry in advance for the shots at the doctor's office tomorrow.

June 16: Baby Dents

There have been a number of occasions, especially over the past year, when we would get a package in the mail only to find that it had been battered and dented while in transit to our doorstep. I have had to make countless calls because of this but it has usually been remedied by the time all is said and done. However, we did receive one gift this year that came to us a little dented but we didn't care. Actually, it was completely normal.

Anyone who has seen a newborn knows what I am talking about. They come into this world a little oddly shaped and with a few dents in their head that make you wonder. Over time, things smooth out but some of the indents are slower to go away than others. So much so that a topographer might go insane trying to update the changing cranial landscape so frequently.

Every once in a while I still look at our son's head and can't help but thinking "that looks like it hurts." I know if my head looked like that I would probably be drooling on myself and crapping my pants too. But it is all part of the developmental process and the thought quickly goes away. It is just odd to see little dents where his head is still forming. I like to think that his head has to work a little bit harder to make room for his huge brain… he is a smart little baby after all.

There are also other things that are still developing while his muscles slowly displace his insulation. Heck, daddy might not have a six pack but baby certainly does. It is actually surprising how strong that our son has become and how quickly his coordination is developing. It is a daily occurrence to find him doing different things and being able to better understand what is happening around him. It is sometimes hard to keep track but it is fun trying to keep up with him.

But even with all of these things changing around him and the development progressing faster than anyone anticipated, those odd little dents in his head remain. He also remains in my eyes to be the perfect baby (I will enjoy this while it lasts). And while I have returned packages in the past with similar dents, our baby is perfect in his imperfections and there is no way I could even consider life without him.

JUNE 18: COMMON QUESTIONS

Every other day it seems I am asked the questions of "how are you adjusting to being a dad" or "what it is like to be a father" or some other similar query. Well, there have been times when I have wanted to pull my hair out when I am either inundated with texts at the office or I am unable to comfort him. While there is nothing better than seeing him smile, there is nothing worse than watching that bottom lip slowly protrude. What can I say, I'm a sucker.

Things have certainly changed over the past year. Our schedules have changed, our lifestyle has been greatly altered, and our priorities have shifted. I am spending more time at home and making sure to spend as much time as I possibly can with our son. Sometimes, I admit, it has been to the detriment of spending quality time with my wife. This is something I am still working on.

It has been a great motivator knowing that we are the ones to care for and raise a child. I begin the day (still not a morning person) with greater purpose but also do my best to minimize the amount of work that I bring home with me. It is a complete shift in how I used to go about each day. I still work a lot but I try to segregate that time and get those other things done after he has gone to bed for the night.

It really is an amazing feeling seeing my son in the morning and being the first one he sees some days as he turns his head and rubs his eyes. Again, that smile is the best way to start the day. It is hard to leave in the morning and say goodbye but I also have a family to look forward to seeing as the sun slowly sinks behind the trees in the evening.

Each and every day, there is something else that I look forward to sharing with my son. It varies each day. Sometimes I see something interesting, find a family document, visit or remember a picturesque place, or even something as simple as going to lodge or attending some other event. We have the plans in place already to share these things with him but the list keeps getting longer and longer as our memories are collected on paper.

And this weekend (and this summer), we will continue sharing those experiences with him.

So, to go back to the question, I think I am adjusting pretty well to being a father. Sometimes I just have to hold on and enjoy the ride but there are moments when I am able to collect myself and make necessary changes. There are a number of things that I still have to work at but I hope to do a better job as both a father and a husband as time goes by. After all, there are a lot of things that we have to cover in a short period of time (which is already going by way too fast).

JUNE 21: ENJOYING THE DAY AND DRIVING HOME

I woke up this morning in a Pittsburgh hotel room looking forward to getting up and seeing my son smiling back at me from his temporary bed. After all, he is the reason for why this day is so special and why I have been waiting for this day for such a long time. What I wasn't expecting was the gift that my wife and my son made for me. It may not seem like much to those without kids but having a picture and hand impression to put on my desk is something that I will always cherish. I really wish I had done the same thing for my wife last month… I guess the distraction was enough of a gift then as it is now.

It wasn't long before we were up, packed, and heading down to the front desk to check out. It was going to be a long day of touring and driving but one that I have been eagerly anticipating. After another quick breakfast in the lobby, we started the day by returning to Station Square. Yesterday, we had planned out the day and knew that we could pick up the tour bus at this location. With a long drive ahead of us we didn't have a lot of time so the best way to see as much of the city as possible was to take the two hour tour on the double decker bus.

Our timing was pretty good and we were able to depart about twenty minutes after buying our tickets. This gave us enough time for a quick diaper change and allowed me to call my dad and wish him a happy father's day. The bus was wide open with only about a dozen people on the top deck and the entire lower level to ourselves. The views might not have been as good but we spread everything out and kept our son out of the sun for the duration. It also helped when it came time to feed him during one of the extended stops.

The tour covered the entire city and while we didn't have a chance to get out and explore we were able to see the stadiums, museums, schools, neighborhoods, and bridges. All the while, we were entertained by the nervousness of the first time tour guide. He did a decent job especially given the script that he had to work with. One thing that we did notice was that the city is in a heavy state of construction/repair. In addition to the horrendous roads throughout the area, there were countless buildings being raised downtown.

By the time we arrived back to our departure point it was time for lunch... the last thing that we would do before heading home. We had already previously eliminated a number of options so we decided to do something a little different and make our own meal... so off we went to the Melting Pot, a fondue restaurant that we passed on our way to a book store the day before. It really was something different and the Father's Day special that they had was something that was just right... I even got a gift certificate during our meal from the manager just for the heck of it. It was an excellent meal and experience (even with our son making is presence known) and it definitely filled us up for the trek back across the Commonwealth.

The long ride home was uneventful as I was able to set the cruise control and turn on some music as my wife and son slept in the back seat. We made pretty good time and the scenery seemed to fly by faster than the confines of time would allow.

Back home, we unpacked the car and carried our son into the house. I will never forget the look on his face when we told him that we were home... obviously he wasn't done yet. I guess he enjoys exploring just as much as his daddy... that really was another great gift that I received on this my first Father's Day.

JUNE 22: LESSONS LEARNED

We have now traveled with our son a few times with this past weekend being both the greatest distance that we have traveled from home and also for the longest duration. I can't say that everything was perfect during these weekend adventures but we were able to get there and back in one piece each time so I would call them successful. However, there have been a few takeaways from our travels thus far and here are just a few of them:

- **Rest Stops Are Your Friends** – Always be cognizant of the rest stops during your drive. Know when you pass one and how long it is until the next one. You may not need to stop at that exact moment but things can change in a matter of minutes.

- **Stick As Closely To His Schedule As Possible** – The last thing you want is your son being in a different and unfamiliar place and have his schedule messed up. Keeping to a feeding schedule as much as possible and repeating the nighttime routine can make things a lot easier.

- **Don't Underestimate The Number Of Wipes You Need** – This is both for the obvious reasons but also because you'll have other uses for them as well. If you are like our family you will be out and about all day… use the wipes to clean your hands regularly. They are also convenient for the occasional road trip spill in the car.

- **You Are Going To Forget Things** – Begin with packing the things that you can't readily replace. Everything else comes after. It is pretty much guaranteed that you are going to forget things so make sure that they are items that you can pick up on the road.

Of course, there are countless other lessons learned during our explorations but those seem to be the four that most readily come to mind. While those might be the things that didn't go as smoothly as expected, there were also things that we were very thankful for as we drove down the highway. Most notably is the fact that we upgraded our cars over the past few months.

While absolutely possible to travel in our former vehicles, having the Outback and the Cherokee have made things a heck of a lot easier.

So this is just the beginning. I am sure that we will make more mistakes and overlook things in the future but we are at least keeping things moving in the right direction. The true test will be next month as we significantly extend our vacation…. I even took time off from work for this one. While there is always going to be some trepidation, I am looking forward to rediscovering a place (and reconnecting with distant relatives) from my childhood and sharing that experience with my wife and my son.

JUNE 23: GUILTY GRIN

The highlight for me almost every morning is walking into our son's bedroom, turning off the music, and welcoming him to a new day. Most of the time, no matter how much he is fussing, when he hears my voice and turns his head he gives me a wide smile and a light in his eyes that make the grogginess of the hour immediately disappear. It is a moment that I look forward to every single day and what allows me to begin the day anew no matter what the previous day had been like.

Of course, there are also the times when I am slightly taken aback when that smile turns quickly into a guilty grim piercing the emanation rising from his crib. Sometimes it is nothing more than air while other times it is a much more pungent and persistent odor that requires immediate attention. Sadly I must admit that he gets that smirk from his daddy as I know all too well what it means no matter if a toxic cloud is present or not.

This reaction has only become more entertaining as time has gone by and our son had continued to grow. Now the questions of "did you fart?" or "did you poop?" elicit that same complicit expression. It seems as though he already comprehends the humor that those bodily functions can bring to a situation (along with the stink). But those are not the only times that this expression appears.

One thing that annoys my wife from time to time is the fact that our son seemingly saves some of his energy toward the end of the day so that he can play when daddy gets home. There have been several occasions when my wife would have a particularly rough day with our son not wanting to cooperate but when I open the door and he hears my voice, our son's demeanor completely changes. I would be lying if I said that I didn't like the fact that he reacts to me in that way but, at the same time, I can see how it can be a little annoying (to say the least) for my wife.

When I sit him on my lap and talk to him about it usually asking if he had been a good boy today, that same guilty grin appears. Except this time he usually drives it home with some cooing and baby gibberish. The force is definitely strong with this one as neither of us can really remain completely annoyed at that point with such effervescent cuteness… this is not the guilty baby you are looking for. At least when this guilt grin appears we don't have to deal with the same fallout that fills the morning.

June 29: More Stuff

When our son was born we experienced a massive influx of stuff. Actually, it started well before his arrival basically as soon as we moved into our current rental. Since the time we began unpacking, it seems as though there is something new that comes through the door just about every week. Sometimes even multiple times a week. While it does add to the massive amount of stuff contained within the walls of our home, we remain grateful for each and every one of the gift that we have received.

Of course, this is all in addition to the things that we find ourselves buying for our son as well. You could even say that we are on the verge of having a serious problem with the number of things that we buy for our baby. The things we buy aren't expensive, they are just the little toys, outfits, and other things that we happen to see in the store or online. Some of them have proven to be necessities while others are far from that definition. Sometimes we just can't help it and find ourselves coming home from a weekend breakfast with one or two small items from the shop next to the restaurant.

Obviously, we are not the only ones as we have found that there are people on both sides of our families that have the same 'problem'. Every time we go to a family event, party, or get together, we leave with more bags than that which we arrived. Again, nothing over the top, just the small toys and outfits that others see in the store and can't resist spoiling our son.

The funny thing is that with each small item I purchase for him he usually ends up with a little money in the bank as well. Especially lately I have found myself paying for things in cash. While I keep a good stockpile of quarters in the car all of the other change goes into his little bank on his bookshelf multiple times per week. I have always had the habit of doing this but now at least it is contributing to something more than just a 'fun fund'.

The house remains the same size while the amount of stuff within the walls continues to grow. We knew that we would be getting a lot of gifts around the time he was born but we didn't expect this much or for it to go on for this long. After all, he is only just over 4 months old at this point. I just hope that we doesn't expect this same generosity to continue when he gets older and given his current indifference to gifts there is a good chance that will be the case.

June 30: Waiting For Daddy

One of the things that I didn't think about when I decided on my new car was the sound that it makes when I lock it after getting home at night. It is a rather inconsequential attribute and I frankly didn't care but I wasn't thinking about how that sound was associated with my return home. With the Malibu, my son had gotten used to the sound it made when I locked the car. He knew that I was home when he heard the noise. Thankfully, the Cherokee makes a very similar sound.

While there are many nights when my car gives away my arrival, there are a several evenings when he is oblivious to my walking through the front door. This is usually the case when he is fussing or sleeping. If he is awake, as soon as he hears my voice he begins looking around trying to find me. It is quite the cute sight. Once he sees me, his eyes brighten and he gives me a big smile (unless he is particularly grumpy that day). I don't care what kind of day I have had up until then, it is a good day from that point forward.

Because she sees this every work day, this kind of annoys my wife. However, this past weekend I was able to be on the other end of the situation as I watched our son during the day while my wife ran some errands that she had been meaning to get to. Our son was not happy to see his mommy leave but I was able to keep him active and occupied while she was gone. As soon as I heard her pull up and lock the car, I let our baby know, and the search began. As soon as she walked through the door and he turned his head, the same bright eyed smile surfaced.

So I guess we are doing okay so far. Our son looks forward to seeing each of us and misses his mommy and daddy when they have to go out for a while. It makes me think about how hard it is going to be when we put him in daycare and, down the road, when we send him off to school. At the same time, I can still look forward to that smile and the ensuing cooing when we are reunited at the end of the day. That is, of course, if I don't screw up between now and then.

July 4: Our Family Was Here

I can't say I have ever been one for big Independence Day celebrations. I have watched the fireworks from a variety of vantage points from the comfort of the living room on the television screen, in Philadelphia, at the New Jersey shore, at my Aunt and Uncle's house, and while lying on the grass in my BDUs in central Missouri. However, while the temporary bright lights in the sky were never something that really interested me a lot, the day has always had tremendous meaning. While I didn't quite understand it early in life, there was still always something a little different about the day.

Of course, now I have a much more complete understanding of what makes this day such a big part of who I am. And I am not talking about the reasons that this day is important to us all, I am talking about the connection that I have, that my family has, to this day and what generations have done since to defend this country. And with those thoughts fresh in my mind, it was particularly special to celebrate this holiday with family, with the whole family, as we gathered together this weekend in Virginia.

And when I say the whole family I really mean it. This is a little different than what usually comes to mind when someone mentions a family reunion. This is not simply the immediate members that you see here and there, this particular reunion brings together all those who can trace back their genealogy to our original immigrant ancestor, Jacob Duffordt, who arrived at the Port of Philadelphia aboard the Hero on the 27th of October 1764. There are thousands in our tree with a small sampling making the trip this year to the mountains of Virginia.

As you can tell by the date, we were here before the revolution and beginning with the simple act of Jacob Duffordt selling supplies to the Continental Army, we have taken an active role in supporting and defending this country. From Jacob Duffordt during the Revolution, to his grandson during the War of 1812, countless relatives during the Civil War, my grandfather and his siblings during World War II, my father in Vietnam, and others in the family who have served more recently. All have given of themselves to ensure that this holiday remains as a day to be celebrated.

Celebrating this day with family, with multiple generations, in a place near where we originally settled is what this holiday is about for me. This was about as close to a perfect representation of the holiday that I can recall and one that I hope to relive many times over in the future. This is our holiday, part of our history, and a reminder of all the generations that came before us and the ones that still lay ahead. We have to remember our history and continue to pass on what we have learned and the experiences we have had so that future generations can look back on this day and experience the same connection.

July 21: Still Recovering

It has been just over a week and we are all still recovering from our summer excursion. While our feet have recovered and our schedules seem to be back to near normal there are still times of adjustment throughout the day. Also, having now been able to think about the trip and trying to get back to our routine, for the record, our son's maximum vacation length is eight days.

Since our return there have been times when we don't want to do anything or go anywhere and there are other moments when we look for things to do and places to go. The same can be said for all three of us as, every once in a while, I catch those looks on my son's face when I know he wants to be out seeing something new. Of course, he still has the occasional moment of "where the heck am I" and "where are we going today?"

There are a lot of things that are back to normal but there are the hiccups that come with change. There are moments when our son is a little more temperamental with his eating or stubbornly not wanting to go to bed. And, with how much he grew during our week away, there are other things that need to be adjusted as well. However, all in all, he has been great getting back into many of the usual routines that he enjoys. It is definitely easier on my wife not having to carry so much stuff around and find new places to feed and change him.

It has certainly been an adjustment from seeing new things every day, being with each other all day, and not having to go to work in the morning but we are working through the change back to normal. Thankfully, in addition to being able to get caught up at work, much of the house work has been done that we put off until we got back. It is looking pretty good actually. Coming home to some of the messy things after being in clean hotel rooms was a bit of an eye opener… we are working on a better daily/weekly routine to make sure that doesn't happen again!

While this summer has gone about as smoothly as we could have ever hoped, I know that there are few things that we have learned along the way and that next summer will be structured quite differently. It has been good to get away and spend time with family but the length and frequency of the trips will have to be adjusted moving forward. This most recent trip was a tad too long while the other ones could have been extended by a couple of days. All lessons that we will apply moving forward.

July 28: Attempt Number Two

By the time Thursday rolled around last week we were finally getting our son back to his daily routine. It had taken some effort after our week and a half long trek through Virginia but we were getting things back to the usual daily routine. His sleep schedule was returning to normal, his wasn't fighting his naps as much, his minor medication has been adjusted to accommodate his recent growth, and his happy demeanor was evident in the smile on his face. Everything was almost back to normal by the time my wife left for the shore on Thursday morning.

Throughout the short time near the Atlantic Ocean, our son took a few steps back. His appetite changed on a nearly hourly basis, he wasn't sleeping, and his 'movements' were unpredictable. This of course changed his whole demeanor during the day and kept both of us, more so my wife, from getting a good night of sleep... this was on top of the fact that my wife and I are not really beach people to begin with and we were once again looking forward to the comforts of home. After our son's experience, it is safe to say that none of us are really beach people.

Once we walked through the door on Sunday, we immediately noticed a change in his mood. He was happy to be home... just the three of us... and enjoyed playing with his toys for the better part of an hour before giving us the look that he was getting bored. At that point he was perfectly happy to lay beside mommy and daddy playing with his blanket and clutching our fingers as he yawned. But while some things improved immediately, other things were obviously still a little off. That yawning and eye rubbing was happening around 6:00... he was ready for bed and soon after let us know how much he wanted to be back in his own room and tucked into his own crib.

That first night back he went to bed two hours early, at 6:30pm, and woke up an hour late, at 8:30am, the following morning. Things are obviously off. So now we are having to get our son back to his normal routine... again! We are slowly readjusting his sleep, doing our best to calm him for his naps, and trying to get the eating schedule back to where it once was. It is one of those Groundhog Day moments when you know things are going to get better and move on but, when in the moment, they seem to take forever. Slowly, very slowly, we will return to his normal routine.

AUGUST 4: POWER OUTAGE

As I was getting ready for bed last night I could hear the wind screaming against the windows and doings it's best Jethro Tull impression with our chimney. I guess we were on the wrong end of the thirty percent chance of rain. The wind continued with relentless gusts as my wife and I recounted the day and not long after we both shut our eyes the room went completely dark. With echoes of thunder and strobes of lightening filling every corner of the house, we knew that this was going to be one storm that our son was not going to be able to sleep through. Just as we finished vocalizing that thought our son proved us right.

He was already having some issues staying asleep lately and this meteorological front was the final piece in ensuring that he completely woke up from his peaceful slumber. We could hear him rustling in his crib between the rumbles and as the rain pelted the roof and the waterfall filled the windowsill, he became more and more vocal. As soon as the crying overpowered nature, we knew it was time to comfort him so we got up, rummaged in the nightstand for a flashlight, and prepared for the long night.

As soon as we walked into the room and began trying to sooth him he calmed down and went back to sleep (well, maybe the second time). What ended up getting him was the fact that the electric decided to start stimming, turning on for a second or two every five or ten minutes for about an hour... just enough to wake him up. The other thing that wasn't helping was the fact that our son was beginning to overheat. He is a little space heater and needs to be kept cool so he was stripped down to a single layer for the night.

Surprisingly, PECO was actually pretty close to their estimate from earlier in the evening as power was restored two hours later. At that point we could all rest a little better and we hoped that we would be able to recover relatively quickly in the morning. It was already going to be a long day for us and now we just added lack of sleep to the mix. It looks like it is going to be a late morning and early night for all of us… it was actually the first morning that I can remember our son not greeting me with a wide smile. Instead, I got a nearly silent snore.

AUGUST 11: WANTING TO WALK

For over two months now our son has expressed his desire to walk. As soon as we get him up and on his feet he starts taking steps. It really doesn't matter where he is whether it be on the couch, the floor, or on a table in Cabela's, he is always trying to get those darn legs to work. Sometimes he actually gets a little frustrated when things don't go according to plan or if he is too tired and his legs don't want to cooperate.

However, over the past couple of months he has gotten better. He is almost ready to support himself as there have been a number of occasions when I am barely supporting him as he stands there. Heck, he is even getting pretty good at doing squats. This kid is almost ready for boot camp (I am pretty sure he could achieve the minimum score on the ASVAB) if he could just make some more progress with his crawling.

While most kids are starting to explore the motions involved with crawling, our son wants nothing to do with them. He would much rather be on his back doing flutter kicks than on his belly shuffling across the floor. It is actually quite entertaining to watch and explains why he already has a baby six pack (note that this turns into a keg by the end of every meal… actually it is more like he wakes up with the six pack and goes to bed with a keg).

After a few minutes of kicking on his back he usually ends up pulling his feet toward his face with toes firmly in his grasp. You know what that means. That's right, this is prime baby boom position and the rapid fire rocking usually produces a mighty breeze. With the kraken now released, the kicking resumes. At this point all you can do is try to keep yourself from falling over from laughter.

It has actually taken some considerable effort to get him to be even remotely interested in the act of crawling and he is now finally getting comfortable on his stomach. This is a whole different round of entertainment these days as he pushes up with his arms and sticks his butt in the air but can't seem to get his legs going at the same time. Maybe the joke is on us and he is actually practicing doing the worn. I guess we will have to find out.

AUGUST 15: HALF YEAR AT LUDICROUS SPEED

When our son was first born people kept telling us to enjoy this time in our life as it will go by faster than we could imagine. While there were some long days here and there that common sentiment holds true as the past six months have gone by at ludicrous speed. Things have certainly changed and it is hard to imagine that our growing boy was once so small trying to grasp my finger as the nurse bathed him for the first time.

Soon our son will be heading off to daycare as my wife returns to work and we hope to have a new (and permanent) place to live in the very near future. There are changes that are fast approaching and I can't imagine that the next six month will move any slower than the last half year. I'm just glad that we heeded that early advice and have done all that we could to take in each and every moment by spending as much time as we could with our son. A routine that we look forward to continuing as the days, weeks, and months slowly slip by.

While he has yet to speak a coherent word (he sounds like a drunk talking to his imaginary friend right now) he keeps trying and it is only a matter of time before he surprises us both with an as of yet unknown first word (hopefully not a Focker moment). It is one of those moments that will seem like it takes forever to happen but will actually go by so quickly that we will once again wonder where the time went. This seems to be the case with all of his milestones, major and minor.

It has already been six months and there are definitely things that we could have done differently and times when I wish I was able to be there but there is also a plethora of memories that I will cherish forever, those moments when I made sure I was there, the times during the daily routine that makes the day just a little bit better (and sometimes stinky). One would think that all of those smiles and laughs would begin running together by now but that is certainly not the case as each morning, each laugh, and each smile at his daddy, remains as vivid as the moment it happened. Six months later and I am more excited to be a dad with every new day that passes.

August 18: 'Tis The Season of Swamp Butt

During the colder winter months and even into the slightly warmer spring, the aroma that filled the car during our son's moments of colonic expression weren't really that bad. When they happened we had a little time to get where we needed to go before changing him. However, as the weather has gotten warmer and the sweltering sun beats through the window during these late summer months, the window of opportunity is much smaller before we begin gasping for air. There have been more than a few occasions when a window had to be opened.

Such is the dilemma during this season of swamp butt. While we want to get to where we need to be as soon as possible, the smell that permeates every crevice of the car at times prevents us from staying on the road. There have been some interesting stops in the past couple of months from small dirt patches on the side of the road to all kinds of parking lots. We have actually become quite adept at spotting a clearing in the distance where we know we can stop, open the hatch in the back, pull the stroller out, and get the job done on the all-weather mats (something I am glad that we got for each of our cars).

There are even times when our son gets a look on his face that shows that even he is a little disturbed by the smell rising up from his car seat and swirling around in the cabin. Sometimes he can smell the swamp butt before the wave hits us. This is particularly interesting given the fact that he is becoming more aware of his surroundings with every passing day. Even while we have been house hunting, there were a few moments of stink when the next stop seemed so far away despite our appointments being so close together.

So, for all the new parents out there I would like to leave you with a little jingle to which we can all relate during these summer months when the sun wreaks havoc on the senses and our eyes water as we search for the nearest place to pull over…

Deck the car with bowels of dookie,
Fa la la la la la la la la.
'Tis the season to be stinky,
Fa la la la la la la la la.
Don we now our stained apparel
Troll the summer colonic carol,
Fa la la la la la la la la.

AUGUST 20: MONDAY MORNING PUKING AND CRYING

It was an interesting way to start the week as I was fortunate to join my wife for our son's six month at the pediatrician's office down the street. We did our best to schedule the appointment early enough so that this would be a possibility and, up until Friday afternoon last week, this was seeming more like an impossibility... thankfully an important meeting got moved without me having to say anything. So, with everything working out logistically, instead of arriving at the office around ten until nine, we were walking into the waiting room watching our son turning his head back and forth trying to take everything in.

Now, I have to be honest about what I feel as we walk into these appointments (beyond the feelings of frustration when they take way too long). I have mixed emotions about going to these appointments. On the one hand I want to support my wife and be there for my son while on the other, selfish, hand I can't stand seeing my baby boy crying in pain.

While I wouldn't say that he is happy to be there, he has at least gotten to the point where he tolerates going to see the doctor and he is actually pretty happy and smiling at everyone until one of two things happens... being naked or getting shots. He wasn't even phased when he threw up on me taking him to the scale or throwing up on my wife as she was bringing him back to the examination room. He is an equal opportunity chucker.

Even with the spewing, it was fun watching my wife's face when the doctor confirmed that he was only half a pound away from 20 and well on his way to being taller than mommy. He is a big boy but, more importantly, he is a healthy baby and one that surprised the doctor by what he is already able to do. While there are a few areas where he is not really excelling in (not really behind either), the doctor was surprised at how advanced his hand eye coordination had become as well as his ability to self sooth.

All of that pretty much went to pot once the vaccine and needles came out. In addition to the nasty taste in his mouth he also left the appointment with two sore legs. But now he is all ready for day care although I don't think that my wife and I are fully ready for that change as of yet. However, I will say that this time around he calmed down much faster and the tears stopped by the time we walked back around to the front desk. Needless to say, it was a tiring morning for all of us and afterward my wife and son went back home while I made some phone calls on my way to the office.

AUGUST 25: HOLDING BACK

Our son is one of those babies that enjoys being out of the house. He likes being in the car (for the most part), visiting new places, and being around most people. It is nice to see him be so outgoing and we try to get him out of the confines of our house and around other people as often as we can. The simple fact that our son is so outgoing made it just a little easier when we decided to put him in daycare.

Today was his first day and while his personality made it a little easier for him, it was still hard for my wife and me to leave him there for the day. He didn't shed a single tear or really seem phased by this new environment as his curiosity had him looking around the room and searching for other babies with which to "talk". It was kind of a surreal experience that left us wondering where the last six months had gone and how our son could already have gotten so big.

While we have left him in the care of family in the past to watch him, this was the first time that we parted ways and entrusted his safety to strangers. We had met them in the past but not for very long. However, we were familiar with the daycare and knew of others who have their kids there so we made the decision to ensure that he is able to socialize while my wife and I are at work. Of course, that didn't keep us from wondering and worrying throughout the day and making a couple of calls to check in on him.

At the end of the day we were both able to pick him up (I spent the day home from work with a headache probably caused from stress and a lack of sleep). As soon as our son heard our voices we could see the smile overtake his adorable face. Again, no crying or fussing, he was just happy to see mommy and daddy again after spending a day with his new friends.

As soon as we left the building we knew that our son was holding back all day as the gas and poop flowed freely now that he was back home. I guess he already knows not to burp and fart in public. Having spent the day apart they were welcomed sounds as we held our son although I could still go without the smells. One day down and a new routine started.

September 1: What Rhymes With Poop?

Well, the poop hit the fan last weekend! As last week came to an end, we were all tired. It was a long week at the office for me, my wife returned to work after doggedly pursuing the last document she needed from a former employer, and our son had his first experience at daycare (he spent three days there). We were all ready for a quiet weekend spent at home taking a break from the chaotic days that seem to have dominated these days off during the summer. Well, that was the plan…

We had noticed that our son wasn't feeling well later in the week and my wife had taken him to the pediatrician on Friday to get checked out. We followed the directions they gave us and we put him to bed with a little Tylenol (per the instructions we were given), a cold air humidifier in the corner, and the head of his bed slightly elevated. A few hours later, with my wife and son now both asleep, I was at my computer sorting through my neglected emails when I could hear what sounded like a wounded cow near the top of the stairs. When I turned the corner to walk toward the bedroom there was my wife holding our moaning child. Something wasn't right.

It wasn't long before we were all in the car on our way to the emergency room. Thankfully, it was a slow night and I was able to hold my son in the hospital bed shortly after our arrival. In the end it wasn't just a cold as the pediatrician told us earlier, he had Croup. Almost immediately after he was given the right medicine the groans stopped and we could both tell that he was beginning to feel better. An hour after we arrived we were back in the car and on our way home. We were all exhausted and soon after our return assumed our positions from before this whole ordeal began.

Obviously we all slept in on Saturday as we resumed our plans and took it easy allowing our son to sleep as much as he needed while my wife and I tried to relax by ordering dinner and simply spending some time together. Well, dinner was a mistake. By Sunday morning our son was returning to his normal happy self while my wife and I were struggling to do just about anything. After my wife reluctantly cancelled her plans for the day, we knew that this wasn't going to get better without some help so we both headed over to the local Urgent Care once my mom arrived to watch our recuperating baby.

Fortunately, the doctors knew exactly how to treat food poisoning and so after some medicine and two IV bags, we returned to the house feeling a lot better than when we left. While we were both nowhere near 'better' we both felt good enough to return to work the following morning and our son, no longer contagious, returned to daycare. It was a long weekend after a long week and I hope we never have to go through that again!

September 3: The Gifts Keep Coming

During the course of the year we have received countless gifts from friends, family, and coworkers for our son. Having now lived through this, I can say that this is the time in life when you see the greatest amount of generosity. The first couple of months of the year saw the greatest deluge of packages and envelopes, but there is still a light trickle of gifts even as we head into the fall. It is pretty amazing the amount of items we have received over the months and we continue to be thankful for each and every item that we receive (even the ones that we return or exchange).

Admittedly, it can be a little daunting at times with the amount of stuff that has accumulated in our house but, in the end, it is all stuff that we have had to purchase anyway. It is interesting to think about the number of things and boxes that we originally moved into the apartment four years ago, the increased amount of stuff that we moved from the apartment to our current house, and the volume that will have to be packed and moved to our next home. And I am sure that the accumulation won't stop there either.

I wish that I was as thoughtful as many of the people that we have in our life. Time and again, I have been presented with the same or similar opportunities and for one reason or another (usually finances or forgetfulness) too long a time passes and the opportunity is gone. I certainly have to get better at this as it is also a time to pay it forward and show the same generosity that has been shown to us. Hopefully there are many more opportunities coming up.

Sometimes I forget about just how great many of the people in our life are and this experience has been a clear reminder of the quality of people that we have in our life. And don't get me wrong, it is not about the numbers. Some of the greatest (and many time most useful) items have been the small thoughtful things that served us well during this learning process. Sometimes it wasn't even a gift. There have been many times when the help or a willing ear have meant a great deal when we needed them. The gifts have only proven even more how much others car about us and our son. That is what it is all about and that is what we try to convey to our son each and every day.

September 8: Welcome to 3AM

While the song has no relation to the situation except for the coincidence of time, I couldn't help by despise Matchbox Twenty this weekend as our son insisted on waking up each night at 3AM. It was a collusion of events last week that caused the constant sleeplessness with his new daycare routine, needing more mommy and daddy time, and the lingering congestion from croup. It was not a fun experience but one that we have been expecting to happen (we actually thought this would be a more regular occurrence during this first year).

Of course, this wasn't the usual stirring in the middle of the night that can be remedied by putting his binkie back in and rubbing his head, this was the "you better not leave me until I am dead to the world asleep" kind of wakeup. Each time he was aroused from slumber, the screaming was almost immediate... it seemed to be a combination of tiredness, frustration, fear, and loneliness. It is a heartbreaking sound to hear echoing through the monitor. However, while I clearly heard each instance, to be honest, it was my wife that was the one that got out of bed to comfort our son while I did my best to keep my eyes open (many times I was unsuccessful).

And this was only the beginning of the fun each day as when the alarm rang out in the morning, it came all too soon and left us all with headaches that persisted throughout the day. Each of us trudged through our days with a set of matching family luggage strapped to our eyes. At this point, I was really hating Cat Stevens as well (or whatever his name is now).

It has been a bit of a testing time for all of us but, as of last night, things seem to be getting a little better as there was no heart wrenching screams to be heard and the remedy for waking up a little earlier than our liking was back to binkie and a quick head rub. The morning was also a bit more pleasant as we were all able to sleep better than we had in weeks.

But the best part about our son feeling better (besides not being woken up at 3AM) was the fact that when I got home from work today his smile and laugh had returned which made me forget, at least briefly, about the recent nights.

September 15: A Lot Of Changes

Another month has passed and once again it feels as though we have been cheated… time is moving so quickly that it is hard to believe that the seasons will soon be changing and our son will be reaching new milestones. With September now upon us, the temperature is getting a little cooler and the Stars Hollow like festivals are popping up all around. It is my favorite time of year made even better by the fact that I can now share the autumn with our baby boy.

The past month has brought a plethora of changes to our little family… actually it has been more of a change in routine than anything. While he has yet to talk, his expressions are becoming even more animated especially when we take him out exploring, drop him off at daycare, and pick him up at the end of the day. He is still a happy baby who likes to be out but also looks forward to spending time with his mommy and daddy at the end of the day.

While the croup from a couple of weeks ago proved to be a slight hiccup (cough actually), he has handled it about as well as we could have ever hoped for. There were some long nights but you could tell that he wasn't happy about being awake either. All the while, the change in the weather (and trying to adjust the temperature) has also been a bit of an inconvenience but one that he has handled well. Unfortunately, while he is doing his best to sleep and rest for the next day, lately he has also become quite the light sleeper like his mommy. This is a whole different batch of issues especially since I am usually the last one up and working downstairs.

It is actually pretty interesting watching him try to get to sleep sometimes as he now likes falling asleep on his side. He has yet to roll over but that too is not far away. One thing he has mastered is sitting up. Whether on the couch, in bed, or on the floor he has been able to sit on his own for more than 30 minutes at a time. This includes catching himself when he begins to tip over and balancing himself when he reaches for some of the thing around him. With the exception of when he is tired, he now prefers sitting and standing. It shouldn't be long before the chasing begins.

And hopefully we will have a new place where we will be chasing him. Maybe not right away but we are trying hard to find the right place for all of us. Some have looked good at the beginning while other require some imagination. In the end, we will be in a place that works for the three of us, a place that we can call home for many years to come. This is a process that has occupied much of the last month and one that our son has tolerated… after all, they have been new places for him to explore.

A lot of changes have happened over the last month but there are even more that we are expecting by the end of the year. He is growing so fast and we are just trying to keep up at this point. Hopefully, the whirlwind will subside soon so that we can enjoy the changes as they float by on the light breeze.

September 29: Rolling

For the past couple of months our son has been rolling over when he feels like it. These moments were usually reserved for the times when we would try to get him to do tummy time... something that he is definitely not fond of. Basically, he wants to be doing just about anything else rather than spend time looking at the ground... although a game of mirror peek-a-boo will usually stave off his escape attempts.

Up until recently he was limited by front to back (also known as the escape plan)... that was before he started teetering on the edge by sleeping on his side. He is usually pretty good about keeping a leg or arm out as a means to stop himself from rolling too far but there have been moments when he forgot to deploy one of these kickstands. A couple of weeks ago he got a little surprise when he accidentally turned a little too much in the crib and ended up on his belly.

We thought that this would cause some level of hysteria but it was actually a pretty calm "oh crap" kind of reaction when it happened. You could kind of see him thinking about how he did it, what he could have done to prevent it, and the fact that maybe it isn't too bad being on his belly when it is his choice. You would think that he would want to practice this but he is back to only doing it when the mood strikes him. Even when we put him on his tummy he still tends to want mommy or daddy to pick him up rather than attempting to roll over.

With that said, it is pretty fun playing with him on the floor and helping him roll from back to front and front to back with very little effort on my part. It should be pretty interesting when the time comes when he rolls a little too fast and ends up in the same position in which he started. I wonder what kind of look will be on his face after that happens for the first time. While there is a chance that he could start crying I am thinking he will just smile and give me a look seemingly asking me "Daddy, how the heck did I do that?" And, of course, no matter which one is his initial reaction, he will probably want to do it again... but only when he feels like it.

October 6: Hi Da Da!

At some point each night, my wife and I try to unsuccessfully prompt our son to say either "ma ma" or "da da". Every night and every weekend it is the same routine. When our son got really sick with croup some weeks back, he was finally able to call for his "ma ma" which alleviated the pounding in our heads just a little bit. It was that sad and touching moment when the two of them connected. He knew that "ma ma" would make things a little better and my wife was able to tear up as he said it for the first, second, and third time throughout the day and night. It also proved that he knows how to say it but chooses to remain a quiet little boy most of the time.

It is because of this that my wife has been pushing more and more for our son to say "da da" as she wants me to have the same experience albeit without the running nose and constant crying (bonus for me). Of course, it is just like our son to say "da da" the moment we stopped pushing him. It was a moment when we were playing on the couch after having been at the office all day and my little boy was just happy to see me. I forget what I had done to make him smile but soon after he said "da da" in such a way that he wanted me to continue keeping him entertained. It was a spontaneous moment for both of us and an instant reinforced of our bond once it happened.

Like many of his achievements thus far he seemed to check it off the list as complete and moved on to the next milestone without any plan on revisiting what he had already accomplished. Hence, I have not heard those simple words since. It was a brief moment but one that will surely remain vivid in my mind for the rest of my life and I look forward to hearing it again when he chooses to do so. Who the heck knows when that will happen again?

I guess this is just another way in which our son is like me, at least that is what my wife thinks. We both tend to check things off the list and almost immediately move on to the next new thing, something that we haven't done before. With that said, we have our routines and there are times when we both revisit our accomplishments especially when they bring a little happiness to those around us. And this little monkey has certainly made us happy.

October 13: I'll Bite Your Finger!

Over the past few weeks our son has been going back and forth between the kind and loving baby that likes laughing and smiling to one that needs to snuggle with his mommy and daddy while a look of pain and fear crossed his face. The later usually coincides with nearly his entire hand shoved in his mouth mere millimeters away from making himself throw up (sometimes he does go too far). We are now in the midst of the teething period when there is little that we can do besides keeping things pressed against his gums and trying to make sure the resulting congestion is cleared away especially during the night.

Most of the time a binkie will suffice but there are moments when there isn't enough pressure and either a cold rolled wash cloth or a knuckle are what he needs to munch on for a few minutes. Even with his teeth slowly protruding further from his gums it doesn't hurt (my wife disagrees with this point) and he is rather entertained by the fact (sometimes) that he is biting daddy. It is hard to watch when he realizes he is in pain and all we want to do is make it go away. In the end there is little that we can do but the things above and the occasional dose of Tylenol… whiskey might have to be next or a Manischewitz lollipop (which did wonders in the past). After all, it would be watered down by all the drool anyway.

Since he now has a couple of teeth that have come in and a couple more trying to break through, we have also added brushing his nubs to the morning and bedtime routines. This is something that is still a little odd for all involved and definitely an activity that our son does not enjoy. But we are all slowly getting used to it and his reaction could be worse like when we try to clip his fingernails… that is a scream I could have lived a full life without hearing.

Also adding to the misery is the constant ebb and flow of various viruses that he either picks up from other babies or things that mommy and daddy happen to carry home from work. All of these things combine to make sleeping a crap shoot and our evenings a test of both patience and endurance. But even when he has those bad days or nights he knows that mommy and daddy are right there to help him and that is really what is important during this time in his life.

October 15: Weathered By The Change

It has now been two thirds of a year and the weather is slowly returning to what it was when our son entered the world. The seasons have changed so quickly that it is hard to believe that soon the slight chill in the breeze will become a bitter wind and we will find ourselves looking out the window at the falling snow thinking about the inches that coated the ground when we left for the hospital that morning. Eight months and a heck of a lot has changed since it was just the two of us.

It certainly hasn't been the easiest experience but it is also one that we wouldn't trade for anything and we now understand the fondness with which people look back on those early months. It may not seem like it at the time, but those days are full of great moments and memories that will undoubtedly continue to fill our minds as our son grows. All the changes and milestones are things that are both surprising when they happen and amazing when we think about how big he has gotten and what he is now able to do all by himself.

Lately it has been a bit of a challenge with the constant colds and teething but it is the brief moments, even glimpses that put things in perspective and make it all worth the bags under our eyes and the fog in our minds. Even now, watching him peacefully sleeping in his crib, all of those tough hours seem to fade away. And knowing that, when we walk up to the crib to get him up tomorrow morning he will give us the biggest smile that his face can handle, all of those instances when we have doubted ourselves will be forgotten. It is the dichotomy that many people tried to explain to us before he was born but that we were unable to fully comprehend until now.

While there were nights and hours that felt like they would last an eternity, eight months has seemed to be but an instant, almost a singular moment in time. Our memories may contradict that sentiment but the reality is that this is all going by so fast... sometimes too fast. If anything, there are times when I wish I could slow down the hands on the clock, look around, and take everything in. Of course, there are also moment that I wish we had a fast forward button but they are definitely outweighed by all the joy and happiness that we get to hug each and every day. Happy 8 months baby!

October 17: Thy Will Be Done!

Before our son was born my wife and I had the conversation that we should really consider getting a basic will put together. It is a subject that has come up from time over the past year but there was always something that would come up to take our attention away from what needed to be done. Finally, at the last stated meeting, I was able to pull one of the brothers aside, who happens to be an estate attorney, and got his contact information. Again, it was a very simple will that we were looking for but something that we now, finally, had the time and opportunity to complete.

The impetus for getting this done really had nothing to do with our financial situation or the possibility of us owning a home in the near future. The motivation was much simpler, we want to make sure, should anything happen to us, that our son would be taken care of by those people that we believe would raise him right and would have his best interests in mind. That is really what we wanted to legally put in place leaving no question as to where he would go and who would take care of him.

The process was actually much easier than we were anticipating as my masonic brother was able to pull everything together in less than a week following my email to him with all the information (names, addresses, special requests, etc.) that were required for these basic drafts. Actually, we had two wills drawn up, one for me and one for my wife. Each mirrored the other as we have been in agreement as to the contents from the beginning. The only difference being that, motivated by previous discussions at the lodge, I specifically requested a masonic service.

Given how easy it was, the fantastic rate which we were charged, and the simple fact that this brother will go above and beyond to assist us and offer us advice, I have already recommended is services many times over to both friends and family. So now the next stop is to the safe deposit box so that we will not have to worry about misplacing the originals. And I must say that it feels great to have this important document now completed and the worry about what we hope will never happen has now substantially subsided. We are now at ease knowing that, should something happen, our son will be taken care of and will be raised the right way.

OCTOBER 20: MY REMOTE!

Our son already has a bad habit. While we keep the television time to a minimum, he still insists on reaching for the remote every time that he thinks that he can grab it. It got to the point that we had to order a toy remote so that he would stop trying to play with the real thing. We even turned the sound off on the toy to make it more realistic (a.k.a. keep us from throwing it out the window and running it over with the car nine or ten times). It works most of the time but, every once in a while, he still reaches for the real thing… he probably knows that the toy is simply a ploy.

It is also interesting to see what shows he enjoys watching. There are a few children's programs that he tolerates (*Chuggington and Mickey Mouse Clubhouse*) but, overall, he likes more of the adult programs especially those that daddy likes to watch too. For our son there is nothing more entertaining than a new episode of *Deadliest Catch* or watching the occasional appearances of Norm Abram on *This Old House*. There are plenty of other shows but the main thing that they all have in common is that he likes the reality programs more than anything else. Not the useless reality shows mind you but the ones where you can tell that he is storing some random knowledge that he will use later in life.

We have tried other shows but there is nothing that really holds his attention. Thankfully, he agrees with daddy that Elmo is probably the most annoying thing to fill the screen. Well, it is at least pretty close to the women on *The View*. Those are the faces that when they show up on the television he either squirms and looks away or he outright screams at the horror that he is now witness to. He is definitely smart beyond his years.

The funny thing is that when there is something on that he doesn't want to watch he puts aside his ploy of a toy and does his best to reach for the real remote. And you better either give it to him or change that channel really fast or the frustration becomes evident in his mood change. Just hope that there isn't a Joy Behar rant going on or you will see him go from calm to crazy at ludicrous speed. And no one wants to see a baby go plaid.

OCTOBER 27: YOUR DINNER LOOKS REALLY GOOD DADDY!

My usual routine at the end of each day is that when I get home I make sure to spend time with our son, play with him, and put him to bed before my wife and I sit down to eat dinner. It may not be the best solution but at this point it is what works and it allows me to spend some time with our baby before having to prep and cook. However, there are times when I get home a little earlier than usual or dinner is particularly quick to pull together and we end up eating immediately after our son finishes his food.

As we are eating we can't help but get the feeling that we are being stared at with every bite. Sure enough, when we look over we see our son watching the food as it travels from the plate to our mouth. This of course is accompanied by copious amounts of drool (more than what his teething usually produces) as well as a smacking of his lips about every other bite. This has been the same routine for months even back to when he couldn't sit up on his own.

Lately, he has taken things to an entirely new level as he really wants to taste what we are eating. At least once during the course of our dinner he will give a little screech and babble something that we are supposed to understand given the expression on his face. Most likely it is probably something along the lines of "Your dinner looks really good Daddy. How about you give me a little taste of whatever it is that you are eating?" He will go on to repeat the babble which is usually concluded by a short burst of yelling when we don't comply.

Thankfully, he is now able to feed himself some small puffs so we usually put some on his tray when we sit down at the table with our plates. This has been much more effective than the small rotation of toys that quickly lose their ability to calm him when food is present. We have also introduced tiny pieces of banana which the three of us are able to share… baby really likes when we are all enjoying the same thing. At the same time, we are slowly introducing him to new foods and broadening his palate so that, one day, hopefully he will like what he tastes when mommy and daddy are able to give him a bite of their food.

November 1: More Sleep?

It used to be that I would look forward to daylight savings time either for the extra hour of sleep or the extra hour of work. Either way, the following morning was just a little bit better. This year, things are a little different. While the potential is still there for an extra hour of sleep it was really more like an extra hour to stay up and get work done. And the morning presented a new slate of issues.

A few weeks back, each of us needing a bit of a respite on the weekends, my wife and I each took a day to sleep in. After a long work week, I preferred to take Saturday morning to remain in bed until 10 while my wife took Sunday to get a little extra rest before the week got started. It is a system that should work well but there are a few hiccups along the way a big one happening this morning.

Our son has been having a few issues sleeping during the week which makes him a little extra tired over the weekend. Of course, it doesn't help that he insists on getting up at the same time each morning no matter what time he fell asleep or if he stayed unconscious during the night. Needless to say, there were a few rough nights leading up to daylight saving time and even though the dial on my watch may have moved back, the timer in our son's head didn't get the memo.

By the time I got him out of bed he seemed a bit out of sorts. It may have only been an hour to many but it made a huge difference to us as we were woken up at the old time. While I always enjoyed the extra hour of rest before, I never truly appreciated that hour until this year. That is a long hour when the bonus time was used to stay awake the night before. Turns out, that wasn't the smartest thing to do.

Of course, the true impact of the time change didn't really hit our son until this evening when what he thought was bed time was approaching... after all the windows had been dark for a while so it must be time to sleep. That was the longest hour of the day. But there were some lessons learned and mental notes taken for next year. Maybe the same mistakes won't happen again when we adjust the clocks in the spring.

November 15: 9 Months

It has only been a month but a lot has changed over that short span of time. Our little boy who once hated being on his belly now enjoys rolling around and flopping on his stomach while trying to reach for a toy. He even lunges at his mommy and daddy when he simply wants to hug or kiss one of us. Of course, that last part is sometimes a little game he likes to play when he is all cuddly and loving one minute and then just goes about playing like nothing happened. When you ask him about it he gives you a momentary smile and goes about what he was doing.

One moment in particular was last weekend when I was taking a break from organizing and all of the sudden, while sitting in the middle of a scattered field of toys, he turned to me and said "daddy". I tried to get him to say it again but it was one of those things that just happened in the moment when he wanted to let me know that he could say it but he chooses not to say it. The weekend prior had a similar moment during the middle of the day when I was laying on the floor next to him while he was playing. Out of nowhere, he turned, leaned over, and gave his daddy about a half dozen kisses. These are just a few of the spontaneous moments that I will always remember.

There are also new routines that have emerged during the last few weeks. Cheerios have become the favorite way to conclude any meal. Not really sure if it is the taste, texture, or the independence that makes them so appealing to our son. Regardless, it is fun to watch him feed himself and play with them a little while sitting in the high chair.

The other regular activity is something that he does when he thinks that no one is watching. Every time that we put him down for a nap or for the night, he spends the first 10 or 15 minutes in his crib trying to crawl. You can tell that he just wants to be more mobile and that he wants to surprise mommy and daddy because while he works on this a bit while we are playing with him it is a completely different intensity when he is all alone with mommy and daddy watching him quietly on the monitor. I guess we should expect another spontaneous moment soon.

November 17: Baby Gets
A Bigger Room

The long day began with our usual morning routine which quickly changed once we got in our cars and met up at our son's daycare. Today we both wanted to be there when we dropped him off as things were going to be quite different when we picked him up. It was a great feeling telling him "You have fun at school, mommy and daddy are going to go get you a bigger room!" From that daycare we drove to another... we haven't been very happy with where our son has been spending his days.

Our appointment began as the last of the children were dropped off by their parents and as soon as we had a moment to sit and look around, we knew that this was a completely different place than where our son was currently spending his time. By the end of the tour there wasn't a question in our mind as to whether we wanted to change his daycare it was all a matter of when would he be able to start. While we were going to make the switch anyway the fact that it was a $100 per week cheaper made that decision a lot easier.

From there we drove up the road a few miles where we met with a brother from the lodge and his wife. It was a relatively quick meeting as we were all running quite a bit behind schedule and before we knew it we were up against the clock to get to our next appointment. We arrived slightly past the time we had hoped to arrive but things seemed to work out as our room wasn't quite ready. This gave us an opportunity to talk with all those who greeted us at the front door. At this point part of me was eager to get things moving while another part was nervous about the changes which were about to occur.

The delays seemed longer in the moment than they do in hindsight. I guess it was all the excitement and anticipation of the day. Looking back it seems like mere moments between the first handshakes to the final signature to the disbursement of checks. While all the leg work and preparations may have been time consuming, it was all worth the effort when we were handed the keys to our new home and our son's bigger bedroom. Now we can finally call ourselves homeowners and now we have a place where we can see ourselves raising our family for many years to come. It is a great new feeling to have especially when you go to pick up your son and tell him that we found a place where he will grow up.

November 24: Getting Used To New Surroundings

Our son was a little thrown off on Friday when he got home from daycare. He woke up in the townhouse and my wife brought him home to our house that same afternoon. Honestly, it was a bit of an odd experience for my wife as well. While there was a bit of an uncertain look in his eyes as my wife carried him through the door, it slowly subsided as we walked him around the house showing him all the rooms (including his bedroom and two playrooms), the variety of windows and views, and the bounty of grass that he will be able to enjoy when the weather gets warmer.

It was an abrupt change for him that first night but one that has gotten easier over the last few days. When we got him up the following morning he was more interested in exploring and less overwhelmed by everything around him. Slowly he became more comfortable and he seemed to come to the realization that we were now home. This is clearest when he is sitting in the playroom downstairs. Every once in a while he will stop playing with his toys, flipping through his books, or trying to pry up the foam letters on the floor and look out the window at the grass and woods behind the property.

Overall, our son seems to have followed in our lead and becoming much more relaxed at home. While there is still a clear adjustment taking place, he is much more active and happier overall. Actually, he seems to enjoy it when we take him around the house now that things are still new yet also familiar.

He is also getting used to the extra space in his room. There is a greater freedom in not having the walls so close and there is less interruptions to his sleep now that mommy and daddy no longer have to sneak by his room to go to bed. Just this simple fact has made a huge difference and, in a certain regard, has proven to be the biggest change to which we have had to adjust.

The important thing is that our son seems to be happy with his new home and my wife and I are happy to have found a home for our son. This is the place where he is going to grow up... but, right now, he is still getting used to it. Of course, what he doesn't know is that there are more changes coming his way next week.

December 1: New School

On the day of our settlement last month we also scheduled a few other appointments because it was going to be one of the few days when both my wife and I were free to take care of things. This is why, before we headed over to the house for the walk through, we had an appointment about five minutes down the road to take a tour of a new daycare. We had a number of issues with the Kindercare where we sent our son and it was time for a change.

Walking through the school it was a completely different experience than what we had been putting up with over the last few months. Even the friendliness with which we were greeted was a welcomed change. By the time our tour was over and having reviewed the curriculum and talking with the teachers, we knew this was a change that was going to have to happen as soon as possible. With little time left in the morning we wrote a check (for substantially less than what we were paying) and took the application with us.

Yesterday, my wife dropped our son off at his new school. By the time I got home from the office I could tell that things had improved tremendously over the previous place. Gone are the days of only sleeping 20 minutes, not being told what was going on during the day, and being challenged with every request that we made. We could tell that he was happier and, having slept for about an hour in both the morning and afternoon, well rested. They gave him his space to fall asleep and they listened to the couple of requests that we had when we started. A completely different experience for us all.

This morning further demonstrated the vast improvement in where our son was spending his day as we looked forward to finishing breakfast, getting in the car, and going to school. Well, at least after he pooped he was looking forward to it. And my wife and I were looking forward to seeing him again at the end of the day knowing that a meltdown wasn't lingering just below the surface. However, one thing did stay the same between the last daycare and this one… he has quickly become the most popular child in the building with all the teachers knowing his name and constantly feeding his baby ego by telling him how adorable he is. Actually, I have to correct all those people, he isn't adorable, he's frickin' adorable!

December 6: Prayers, Candles, and Presents

A couple of nights ago we started Hanukkah a little early. Over the last month we had bought a few too many toys for our son so we figured we would begin part of the evening routine a couple of days prior. He didn't really know what to make of it but he was happy with what we got him and seeing that smile made the few extra dollars seem like the bargain of the century. After all, this is his first Hanukkah and we want to make it a little more special so we have tried to make it as fun as possible while setting the ground work for a new holiday tradition.

We are starting this tradition as a family... just the three of us this year. Throughout the weekend, my wife and I made enough brisket to last for the eight nights and we made sure, beginning tonight, to light the candles with the proper blessings. It is only after the candles are lit, which our son seems to enjoy in and of itself, when we go back into the office closet and pull out the next toy for our son to play with. Reading the transliteration in front of our son knowing that, at one point I could read the Hebrew, reignited my desire to learn this beautiful language.

There is something calming about slowing down for a few moments, reading the prayers, and carefully lighting each candle. It really allows all three of us to just be in the moment while we enjoy our faith as a family. This followed by the happiness in our son's face as he played with the toys (and the boxes that they came in) are really what makes this a special time of year and I look forward to sharing with him more and more about the holiday and the significance that it holds.

Of course, there is also another fun part of the evening as I was able to hide the small gifts that I have been accumulating over the past several weeks from my wife. Well, most of them are small. While the vast majority were clearance finds or daily deals, I was also able to find something that I had been meaning to get for her for some time now. Thankfully the camera that I was looking at went on sale and I was able to stay within budget.

So now, each night, we will have images to accompany our memories and, most importantly, I might have made up, at least a little bit, for my mistakes during her birthday.

And now, with the candles having long since faded, and my wife and son sleeping, I am sitting here writing this and looking forward to the rest of the Hanukkah holiday. I am so glad that we are able to have this experience throughout the week and I can't wait to see the smiles every evening. And, just think, it only gets better from here.

December 8: Thank You Daddy!

A few months back while spending the day with our friends for their son's birthday party, our son found one the toys in their house to be greatly entertaining. It was a stationary car that allowed him to sit on the floor and play with all the buttons, steering wheel, and the other odds and ends that are included on it. He must have spent close to an hour that afternoon entertaining himself while the rest of us ate lunch and caught up in our conversations. It didn't take long before my wife and I realized that was going to be one of his Hanukkah gifts this year.

A couple of weeks ago, before we moved, I got really lucky and found the same car, the only difference was that it was in blue not red, on sale on Amazon. I think it only took me about 10 or 15 seconds from the time I saw it until I had the order placed. A few days later it arrived in an abnormally large box at my office. There it stayed until we got settled in to our new home which, at that point, I moved it into the office closet one night while our son was asleep.

Yesterday, having taken the day off from work, the box finally emerged and while our son was excited enough about the big box he was going to be able to play with, once we were able to put the car together his face lit up as he seemingly recognized the toy that he had enjoyed previously. Just like the first time he saw it, once my wife and I put him in the car he spend at least an hour playing with all the buttons and features occasionally glancing up at the two of us and smiling.

After a while he decided he was done and wanted to squirm around on the floor and play with mommy and daddy. This is not a surprise as any parent will tell you that it doesn't matter how much they like a toy they are going to get bored with it after a while. What we didn't expect was for our son to come after me kissing me, smiling, laughing, and seemingly thanking me for a toy that he really wanted. It was one of the most adorable 10 minutes that I have ever spent with our son and something that I was both not expecting and will never forget. I just feel bad that he didn't do the same for his mommy.

December 15: Baby Hits Double Digits

Our son has officially reached double digits! I have no idea where the last ten months have gone but it is fascinating to think about all the changes that have happened over that time. Our baby is quickly turning into a little boy and all I can think about each day is trying to figure out how to stop time for just a day or two so that I might have an outside chance of catching up and having a moment to breath. But, at the same time, there is little I would change about how the last few months have gone… only one thing really. There have been great moments and difficult nights but, overall, it has been an experience which I wouldn't change for the world.

These monthly milestones always have me thinking about those first few weeks when I was more concerned about breaking him rather than simply enjoying the quite moments holding my sleeping son. It was a time of light pats trying to get the burps out compared to the firm jostles that actually get the job done. Our son was pretty quiet from the very beginning. It may not have seemed like it at times but we have seen the way that other babies scream in restaurants and other public places. And, yes, our son still gives those kids the stink eye for interrupting his day.

It is amazing to think that only ten months ago he was holding my index finger as the nurse was cleaning him off for the first time. Now, it is hard to get him to stay still and when he does grab my hand it is more out of fascination rather than for comfort. Although it is nice to hear him babble rather than crying being his only means of communication.

So much has changed in our baby boy over the last ten months and so much has changed around him as well. However, the most important things are not the changes that have happened but the simple facts that he continues to be the same happy baby today that he was in the beginning, he still smiles at us in the same innocent, and sometimes not so innocent way, and he still finds comfort in our arms. Our son, and the love that we have for him, is growing so fast. No matter how much we love him at any given moment I know that it will increase exponentially over time (at least until he is a teenager). It may not always be easy but life doesn't get much better than in those simple moments shared between a father and a son.

December 22: I Want
To Talk To Daddy NOW!

Part of my daily routine is calling my wife while on my way home after work. I have done this for a while and in the past it wasn't as regular as it has become over the past year. Of course, now my wife and I have little say as to whether my phone is going to ring while I am getting on the highway.

Every day, so I have been told, when my wife picks our son up from work he babbles in the back seat saying "da da" over and over again as if it has become his infant mantra. This usually continues for much of the afternoon (and sometimes into the night) until he finally gets to the point when he reaches for my wife's phone, says "da da", and waves. He may only be ten months old but he has no issues getting his message across... I want to talk to dada now!

This is pretty much the same routine regardless of whether he is having a good day or a bad day and sometimes, for some reason, hearing my voice on the phone is one of the few things that will calm him down. However, consider yourself warned, if he is expecting to talk to daddy and you decide to call, he will not readily accept this and will be rather vocal about his displeasure. I am told that it is an interesting site to behold when the voice on the other end of the line is not that of his daddy... basically, imagine being cursed out in baby babble.

Of course, I am of two minds when I think about this routine that we have and the close relationship that I have been able to build with our son. While he knows my voice and he looks forward to seeing me every night, I am usually only able to spend anywhere between 30 and 60 minutes with him per day. And that is if I don't have anything going on that night. This is why I am happy to have the relationship that we do but, at the same time, I don't like the fact that I see him for such a small amount of time.

It's almost as if I can hear Harry Chapin warming up back stage letting me know that I am walking a fine line. He is ready to go and can start singing at any time if I screw up. That is the last thing that I want to happen and why when I am home I give my son as much attention as I am able, play with him, and tell him I love him whenever I am given the chance. It may not be ideal but, so far, it is seems to maintain the strength of our connection.

December 29: Unusually Warm Weather

When we originally went to settlement on the house we accepted the fact that we probably wouldn't be able to enjoy the outdoor space until the spring. Well, we were definitely wrong in making that assumption as the weather has been oddly warm. Because of this, our son has been able to go outside in little more than a sweatshirt or light coat (at most) and take in the clean air. He has also been able to enjoy looking up at the countless trees which he has done since we first started carrying him outside last spring.

One of his favorite spots in the yard, probably on the entire property including inside, is the gazebo. While he hasn't spent a lot of time in the yard (it still gets dark quickly this time of year) he always has a smile on his face when he is sitting in the middle with one of his toys. And the toy is pretty much secondary as he spends more time looking around and making cute sounds rather than playing. I'm just glad that he likes being outside rather than staying cooped up in the house.

With the warm weather, he also likes having a slight breeze in the car whenever we have to go here or there. It's actually pretty funny, and cute, hearing him take in deep breaths as soon as we crack the back window. Hopefully this doesn't continue once the weather finally realizes that it is supposed to be freaking cold out and the slightest air leak into the car leads to hours of shivering.

At the same time, I am curious to see if our son likes the snow. While he has seen it, he wasn't able to fully process what it was at the time or enjoy watching it flutter through the trees. It should at least be an experience watching his reaction to both the flurries falling from the sky and the resulting blanket across the yard. He would probably enjoy watching everything from the dryness of the gazebo.

It is nice knowing that our son enjoys the outdoors and I am already looking forward to not only his reaction to the snow but the warmth that is supposed to come about with the spring and summer. He should be quite mobile by then and I am looking forward to exploring the property with him. After all, I haven't had a chance to see everything yet either.

2016:
WE MADE IT!

January 5: Holiday Hangover

Having spent the last week and a half at home with my wife, it was quite the change yesterday when we put our son in the car and had him spend the day at daycare. While he has been getting up at the same time regardless of the plans for that particular day, the morning routine was a little more hectic than it had been the previous week which didn't really phase our son as he continued to take his time savoring every breakfast Cheerio. By the time we got his coat on, he knew that we were going back to our usual routine and he actually seemed to be okay with the switch.

Heading out in the morning wasn't that much of a change as we try to get him out of the house regularly. However, when he is home all day, he works at a much more leisurely pace when it comes to eating. He tends to pick for at least 30 minutes rather than simply shoving food into his mouth as fast as he can (the only exception to this would be his Gerber tropical fruit melts). While we did head out the door a little later than we wanted (I know, what a shock) we were at least able to speed him up a little bit and I guess you could say meet in the middle.

We are very lucky in that our son enjoys being at daycare and enjoys being social in general. Of course, he also likes being with mommy and daddy so by the end of the day we had to make sure to give him a little more attention than usual so that he could get his fix before bed. This can sometimes be an issue if he either goes to bed early or his daddy has to be out late but I am usually there to play with him and hold him a little bit before he begins his evening procedures.

There was a bit of a hiccup yesterday with his sleep (or lack thereof to be more accurate) but that will return to normal over time. So we are back to our normal schedule and thankfully it was a pretty smooth transition that first day. Hopefully things continue and he sleeps a little better during day two. Sometimes, transitions just take time and we have to be a little more patient until we can shake the holiday hangover and get used to the old daily routine.

JANUARY 12: CRAWLING

It wasn't long ago when our son figured out how to sit up by himself from his stomach. It was one of those things that my wife and I caught him doing on the camera and soon thereafter he would sit up when he felt like it or, on occasion, when daddy asked him to do it. Heck, that is how I was able to see him do it and the smile that he gave me afterward is something I won't forget. Since then I have been able to ask our son to sit up before picking him up. He's actually pretty good about following directions when he wants to be cooperative.

It seems like just a short time ago when we were enjoying those moments which were soon followed by scooching across the floor and sitting up and lunging in a different direction to get what he wanted. That turned into a quasi-Army crawl which then became a half crawl which primarily propelled him backward. He has moved well past all of those stages and now the forward momentum is taking over. We are in trouble.

It started with a couple steps forward followed thereafter by three or four shuffles back. As the counterproductive kinks got worked out he began moving a little further each time. The toys on the other side of the room weren't so far away after all. Once he could clear the room without stopping he started picking up the pace. This was particularly noticeable when he started catching the battery operated train and cars that he once just looked at as they rolled by.

Now there is a little more purpose with his crawling as he knows to move toward the hallway so he can see daddy walk through the side door when he gets home. He can also crawl to a toy, almost like he is stalking it at times, and reach up with one hand and grab it while still supporting himself. From there he reverts back to an old trick and sits up so he can play with his prey.

I guess this means it is time to really start thinking about the different safety locks and baby gates because he seems determined to move around the house by himself. It is that time already. I don't know how we got to this point so fast but it is time to evaluate and see what needs to be done so we don't hear cabinets slamming on fingers or our son sliding down the stairs like dirty laundry on a wash board. Time for some DIY.

January 16: Another Month Gone, One Month To Go

It is rather astounding to think about how much has changed over the past month. Even with the few challenges that we have encountered with an ear infection, fever, and multiple teeth making their way to the surface, it was a great month that provided us with a number of amazing transformations. Probably the most interesting have been the awareness and cognition that our son seems to have now in comparison to previous months.

When we walk into another room for a minute he understandably gets upset unless we tell him that we will be back in a minute or we keep talking to him while we grab our phone, clothes, computer, etc. When my wife says that Daddy is home, our son looks toward the door and waits to hear it open. Sometimes he will even crawl into the hallway so he can watch daddy walk in. Either way, it is usually accompanied with him waving hi as I walk through the side entrance.

He is also much more mobile now having gone from sliding backward on his belly to crawling circles around his mommy in the playroom and chasing the train as it sings while traversing the playroom. It is a big difference from just a month ago when he took great pride in showing us that he could sit up all by himself. And an even bigger difference from the days when we were waiting to see the first time he would roll over on his own. Things are changing so fast.

Now we are less than a month away from his first birthday. Eleven months and our lives are completely different. I can't believe it has already almost been a year. Given all that happened that day it will undoubtedly be a day of mixed emotions but, above all else, one of disbelief as neither my wife nor I can get around the fact that a year has already passed since our lives took such a drastic change in direction. And that was just the beginning of a year that was probably the most hectic that any of us has ever experienced.

So many changes and differences but, when we look at our son, when we see the smile on his face and hear the joy in his laugh, it is all put in perspective. He is our miracle and he has been the one to get us through the tough moments. Watching him change and grow keeps us on our toes but also pushed us out of bed in the morning with a wonder of what is he going to do next that can't really be put into words. It is an amazing feeling and I can't believe that we have been waking up to that feeling for over eleven months now.

JANUARY 19: SCREAMS IN THE NIGHT

One of the scariest sounds that I have ever heard is when we have been startled from a deep sleep by the screams from our son echoing across the room through the monitor. While my wife's hearing is more in tune with the displeasures of our son, when I am able to remain unconscious to the troubles around us, there are times when it doesn't matter how sound a slumber, the scream that our son makes could wake anyone up… even me!

Just over a week ago this seemed to be the pattern for a few nights as our son spiked a fever well into triple digits. It was a time of little sleep, especially for my wife, as all we could do for a couple of nights was monitor, give him medicine, hold him, and dunk him in the tub if he got too hot. Unfortunately, I am little help during these times as our son insists on having his mommy but will occasionally want his daddy within his sight line. This episode, this sequence of nights, was far beyond those that we have dealt with previously.

Even without a temperature and feeling perfectly fine, there are moments when our son will wake up and make some noise before falling back to sleep. What can I say, he is loud when he shifts just like his daddy. There are also moments when he will fuss or even whimper for a minute or two before he either screams because of some uncomfortable padding under his bottom or he will unleash a different kind of sound that fills the night, lay down, and sleep better than he did before he woke up.

There was also a period of adjustment when we moved into the house when we couldn't quite get the thermostat right… our son has become rather particular with regard to ideal sleeping temperature in his room. Over the first couple of weeks we were able to figure it out. Who am I kidding, my wife is the one that fine-tuned the temperature. And now, if there are nights that are a little warmer or cooler, our son adjusts his position in the crib sleeping either in a slightly cooler spot near the wall or a little warmer away from it.

And while we have done everything that we can to make him as comfortable as possible, sometimes there are nights when he doesn't feel well. Sometimes there are evenings when he is startled by a nightmare (also a scream that is hard to forget). Sometimes he simply loses track of his stuffed animal and/or binkie. And other times there are nights when he gets a little lonely being on the second floor by himself or when we didn't spend enough time playing with him during the day and needs a little more snuggle time with mommy and/or daddy. But these nights are nothing in comparison to that heart wrenching siren.

JANUARY 26: HI SNOW!

One of the fun things about the recent blizzard was that my wife and I were looking forward to introducing our son to some real snow not just the light dusting that we got a couple of weeks ago. Thankfully, as the frozen season descended upon us, our aunt sent our son a snow suit that will keep him warm and my wife picked up some tiny boots last week. We were all ready to go.

As we brought our son down from his bedroom on Saturday morning we made sure to walk over to the window and show him the white blanket across the lawn. He didn't seem too impressed but was rather intrigued as to how different the yard looked. Of course, he did just wake up and we had yet to feed him so nothing is really exciting at that point. However, as he ate his breakfast he kept looking out the window as the sheets of powdered ice blew by the window.

It was a bit too cold to bring him out in the middle of the storm but the following day was different. The snow had stopped the night before and the sun was already starting to melt the tops of the piles. As we brought him down the morning after the storm he once again looked out the window, gave a little smile, and waved hi to the snow. It was the perfect weather and opportunity to introduce him to this winter tradition so we bundled him up and headed out onto the cleared asphalt.

He had a big smile on his face as we carried him around and seemed quite curious when we sat him down atop the two feet lining the driveway. He was happy and even giggling for a few seconds before beginning to squirm onto his belly and his back. While he was entertained a little when daddy helped him make a snow angel, he was over it. Turns out that he likes the way snow looks but would prefer to look at it from the warm side of the glass. Can't say I blame him.

Of course, I am certain this will change over time as sledding enters the picture and, overall, he becomes more active. A time that my wife and I are definitely looking forward to… my wife can take care of the skiing,

I'll take care of the sliding on the rear. But, for now, even though the snow is fun and some would say magical for most kids, our son would much rather wave at the white stuff from the other side of the window. Bye Snow!

February 2: Appointments

It seems that whenever we take our son to the doctor there is always another appointment to be scheduled. Thankfully, he is actually pretty good in the waiting room and even on the examination table so long as we are there and there is plenty of tissue paper to play with. However, the service that we have received from his current pediatrician has fallen far short of the expectations of quality care. The last two appointments are indicative of this level of service.

With our overachieving son deciding to cut about a half dozen teeth at the same time, we have run into a few bumps both during the night and throughout the day. It has interrupted his sleep patterns which have always been pretty good and it has had an impact on his eating. While he is still healthy and generally happy he does have his moments and once things had continued for some time we decided to bring him in to see the doctor. Keep in mind that this was after we called and were told to bring him in to see said doctor if things continued.

While I am not usually a stickler for these things, when I make an appointment to see the doctor, especially when acting upon their own advice, don't give us a hard time making the appointment and make sure that we see the doctor not just someone you call "doctor". On top of that, it would be nice if this "doctor" would follow the same plan as the actual doctor instead of contradicting almost everything that we have been told and arguing with us each time we said anything.

That was just the first example. The second is the fact that one of the nurses, who too frequently handle the appointments, insisted that we take our son to an Ophthalmologist because he would probably need either glasses or a temporary eye patch. I honestly never noticed a lazy eye but we made the appointment to get it checked out and my wife and I spent some time trying to figure out how to deal with this new situation as we waited for the scheduled day to arrive. A couple of weeks ago, we took our son to see the specialist and it didn't take but maybe 10 seconds for him to tell us that there was nothing wrong.

It wasn't even a question... he found nothing. And, while he wasn't about to say anything directly, we had a little conversation about how we should have probably never been sent there. Nice to have a professional back up the opinion that I have already been forming in my head about the current office. Needless to say, it has not been an easy experience and continued to be a difficult process simply getting someone on the phone at times as well as every time we try to schedule an appointment. Goes to show, sometimes the most well-meaning opinions and advice that you received about a place beforehand are, at the very least, subjective and experience is what really matters.

February 9: Standing

I still remember the look of both pride and sheer joy on our son's face when he sat up by himself for the first time. I will always remember the moment when he finally figured out the coordination and started crawling. I continue to look forward to seeing him scurry from the playroom to greet me when I get home after work tugging on my pant leg until I pick him up. And, right now, I hold my breath a little bit every time he pulls himself onto his feet and sways as his legs continue to shake.

That is what he is focusing on now. He has figured out how to stand, how to pull himself up onto his feet, but he isn't the most stable baby at this point. He is getting better but he also isn't about to let go of his support anytime soon. And he hasn't quite mastered the getting up to his feet part yet either. He actually gets pretty frustrated when it takes too many tries to get vertical. The same impatience that was on display when we was still figuring out how to crawl.

It is amazing how much he is able to do already and how much he has changed during the past couple of months. As he tries to do more his personality seems to develop more and more and, at the same time, we can tell that he never wants to settle for what he is able to do right at that moment… he always wants to do more or at least do what he is working on a little better. Meanwhile, my wife and I are simply encouraging him and telling him "good job" as he stands there with his wobbly legs. That is obviously not good enough for him.

Actually, what we are seeing him start to do now that he has been standing for a couple of weeks is that he is starting to almost walk in place. It obviously isn't very smooth and can sometimes cause him to lose his balance but you can tell that he is wanting to really be mobile… even as fast as he has become on all fours, crawling just isn't good enough. We can tell already that he is going to be a handful as he gets older and is able to do more and more. This could get really interesting really soon… glad we finally put up baby gates last weekend!

February 15: One Day Makes A Difference

Even as I type these words and watch them appear on the screen I still can't believe that it has already been a year since we met our son for the first time. Our lives changed in an instant and I can still remember the feeling of shock that originally hit me when my wife's water broke. While I was able to pull myself together, collect most of our things, and drive us down the snow dusted highway to the hospital, that daze didn't really lift until hours later when our son grabbed my finger for comfort as the nurse cleaned him off.

There are moments from that day, and from the week for that matter, that remain a little hazy having melded together in a jumbled memory but there are also moments, good and bad, that remain clear as if they only happened an hour or two ago. That is what makes this passage of time so unbelievable. And while there have been trying moments to be sure during this first year of parenthood, I wouldn't never want to go back to the way things used to be. Being a father, sometimes even a good father, is what I enjoy most each and every day.

It has been an interesting year full of first experiences, difficult moments, and challenging situations. It has been a calendar full of change but one that has brought us to a great place in our lives. There have been the funny moments of dodging poo and casting wee rainbows, nurturing times when our son got sick or was overwhelmed during his growth spurts, and adorable moments when he would smile, laugh, or nuzzle in our arms. And the daily joy beaming from his face, some days it is more prevalent than others, is enough to make even the most difficult days disappear.

Of course, we also find ourselves in the unique position of celebrating and mourning at the same time. While our son's birth and my mother-in-law's passing technically happened on the same day, this is one of the times that I insist on going by the Hebrew calendar. By doing so our son's birthday, the 26th of Sh'vat, 5775, is separated from the date on which my mother-in-law passed away, 27th of Sh'vat, 5775. Having that single day of separation makes a huge difference at times. It is interesting how faith can be comforting in the most obscure ways in addition to the guidance that it provides during times of struggle.

However, while there are no trips to grandma's house that our son will remember about growing up, he still knows his grandma and recognizes her in pictures. It hasn't been easy but there is a bond between the two of them that we both wanted for our children long before our baby became a reality. We didn't plan on it happening this way but the important thing is that they are connected, our son knows his grandma, and his laugh when he sees her picture eases just a little bit of the pain from that day.

And this is just one of the many ways that our son continues to change how we look at life and the world. At times he has been our sole reason for happiness but mostly he has provided us with the love that permeates every moment of life and makes us remember that the love is what we always need to remember. Whether someone is here or not, the love remains. As I have said before, I will forever be thankful for that gift which our son has given us.

It is a complicated day, couple of days actually, but one that comes down to the most simple of statements... Happy 1st Birthday my adorable baby boy! Mommy and daddy love you!

ABOUT THE AUTHOR

Sean M. Teaford has gained a reputation as a talented poet and insightful essayist with honest images that remain with the reader long after the page has been turned. Over the past fifteen years, Sean has published over a hundred poems and over a thousand online articles. He is the author of four books of poetry, two essay collections, and maintains a daily blog, Time To Keep It Simple, which has served as a record of his life as a traveler, writer, genealogist, photographer, Rotarian, Mason, convert to Judaism, and, most importantly, as a husband and new father.

In addition to serving as an editor for a variety of literary publications, including the Endicott Review and Mad Poets Review, he has coordinated numerous poetry readings across the Northeast and has been a featured reader in the Boston and Philadelphia areas. Sean received a M.F.A. in Creative Writing from Rosemont College and a B.A. in English from Endicott College.

A public relations account executive, Sean lives in Morgantown, Pennsylvania with his wife and son.